KiDS' CRAZY CONCOCTiONS

Library of Congress
Cataloging-in-Publication Data

Hauser, Jill Frankel, 1950-
  Kids' crazy concoctions: 50 mysterious mixtures for
art & craft fun / Jill Frankel Hauser
    p.   cm.
  Includes index.
  ISBN: 0-913589-81-0
  1. Handicraft — Juvenile literature. 2. Cookery —
Juvenile literature.
[1. Handicraft. 2. Experiments. 3. Cookery.] I. Title.
TT160.H367 1994
        745.5—dc20   94-4633
                                              CIP
                                              AC

Cover design and illustration: Trezzo-Braren Studio
Interior design: Trezzo-Braren Studio
Illustrations: Loretta Trezzo
Printing: Capital City Press

Williamson Publishing Co.
Box 185
Charlotte, Vermont 05445
1-800-234-8791

Manufactured in the United States of America

10 9 8 7 6 5 4 3

KIDS' CRAZY CONCOCTIONS

50 MYSTERIOUS MIXTURES FOR ART & CRAFT FUN

JILL FRANKEL HAUSER

Illustrated by Loretta Trezzo Braren

CONTENTS

★ DEDICATION ★

To Zev who says, "Do you ever dream for something?
Then make it!"

To Savlan and Emunah — concocters to the core.

And to all grown-ups who throw out the coloring books
and pass out the messy stuff!

★ ACKNOWLEDGMENTS ★

Thank you to those special people from whom I learned about
the fun and power of creative concocting:

Art Department of the University of California at Berkeley

Art Department of California State University at Los Angeles

Barnsdall Art Center in Los Angeles

Shasta College Early Childhood Education Center
in Redding, California

★

Jill Frankel Hauser is also the author of

GROWING UP READING
Learning to Read through Creative Play

available from Williamson Publishing Company

★ MIX UP SOME FUN! ★

Are you the kind of kid who loves to mix, mash, mush, and mold? Do you like to get your feet in mud, paint with eggs, and squish bubbles? If so, fire up your imagination and get ready for some excitement. With the fifty crazy art concoctions plus hundreds of art smart ideas in this book, you can't help but have a great time.

The cave painter searched for just the right rock to grind for pigment. The Renaissance master experimented with egg and oil binders. Van Gogh sought paint with the perfect thick consistency to spread onto his canvas. For each of these artists, making the art material was a key part of the creative process. With such simple household ingredients as flour, water, or soap flakes, you can join in on this centuries-old artistic tradition.

Concocting is more than mixing up a recipe. It's experimenting and exploring. What happens if you add sugar or more water? The best answer is, "Try it and see!" You'll have the most fun through your own creative exploration. The projects following each concoction extend this exploration. No limiting directions here! Just open-ended projects that invite you and your friends to use your crazy concoction in a way best suited to your imagination, your mood, and the concoction's unique attributes. Soon you'll discover that the most important ingredient to add is your own imagination.

So bring out your creative spirit. Concoct a whole new substance. Then, let that substance inspire a masterpiece unique to the qualities of the mixture and to your personal creative expression. Your concoctions can be one of a kind; your creations can be one of a kind — and it's all because YOU are one of a kind!

Where should you begin? Skim through the book to see which concoctions look most intriguing and best suit your mood. Art concoctions are grouped into these sections: paints, papers, pastes, clays and doughs, and earthworks. Is it a great day to be outdoors? Try a mudscape. Is there leftover bread from breakfast? How about mixing up a batch of bread crumb beads. Is old paper piling up? You can blend its fibers with water to make a delicate paper bowl.

Just don't forget to add the most important ingredient of all — your imagination! After each concoction recipe, you'll find a special project to make with your concoction. There's no one way to make it and loads of room for your own creative touch. Let the look and feel of your new mixture inspire you. You'll surprise yourself with an artistic masterpiece all your own.

By the way, just in case you're curious about these mysterious mixtures, you'll find extra information about them in special sections throughout the book.

HELPFUL HINTS

★ Get permission before you start concocting.

★ Protect your work area with old newspaper.

★ Protect your clothing with an apron or big, old shirt.

★ Assemble all ingredients and equipment before you begin. It's no fun to mix the flour and water together only to discover you're out of salt.

★ Clean up your work area and equipment as soon as you are finished. It's much easier to sponge off paint while it's still wet. The same thing is true for getting paint out of brushes.

SUPPLY LIST

All concoctions are made from safe household, or inexpensive, easy-to-find ingredients. Here are some of the items you'll need and where to find them:

GROCERY STORE

★ Flour

★ Salt

★ Sugar

★ Cornstarch

★ Baking soda

★ Food coloring

★ Gelatin

★ Soap flakes

★ Liquid dishwashing soap

★ Liquid starch

HARDWARE STORE

★ Sand

★ White glue

CRAFT STORE

★ Powdered tempera paint

★ Clear acrylic sealer

★ Paintbrushes

★ Art paper

AROUND THE HOUSE

★ Mixing bowl and spoon

★ Measuring spoons and cups

★ Sieve

★ Zipper-style sandwich bags

★ Water

★ Dirt

★ Yarn

★ Scissors (use safety scissors and handle with care)

★ Hole punch

★ Blunt knife

RECYCLED ITEMS

★ Newspaper

★ Airtight food storage containers such as jars and margarine tubs

★ Squeeze catsup or mustard bottles

★ Styrofoam egg cartons to use as paint palettes

★ Paper pulp egg cartons for paper mash

★ Scrap paper for experimentation and handmade paper

★ Cereal and cracker boxes for light-weight cardboard

SAFETY FIRST

★ Get grown-up help when indicated in the instructions. (This is not only for safety; it lets the grown-ups get in on the fun!)

★ Don't put concoctions in your mouth, even if they are made from kitchen ingredients.

★ It's always best to use art materials in a well-ventilated area.

★ Ask a grown-up to help you dispose of molding pastes, doughs, or paints.

★ Do not pour gloppy stuff like thick paint, dough, or paste down the drain. It can clog. Instead, place gloppy stuff in a plastic bag and twist-tie shut. Throw it out in the trash. Or, let gloppy stuff dry hard; then throw it out in the trash.

GLOPPY STUFF

Changing the Quantity

Most recipes make enough for a single kid-sized concocting portion. If you're working with a friend, or you'd like to try more than one project, double the recipe. Maybe you want to sample a concoction by making a small quantity. You can halve the recipe. Here's how:

Castle for Keeps (page 125)

	Sand	Cornstarch	Water
original recipe	2 cups (500 ml)	1 cup (250 ml)	1 cup (250 ml)
double recipe	4 cups (1 l)	2 cups (500 ml)	2 cups (500 ml)
half recipe	1 cup (250 ml)	1/2 cup (125 ml)	1/2 cup (125 ml)

Although you've made more or less of the mixture, the *proportions* (the ratio of the amount of one ingredient to another) are still the same.

Here's another way to change the total quantity of the mixture without changing the proportions. Notice how this recipe is given in cups or milliliters. Your cup, or measuring device, can be any size. This recipe calls for equal amounts of cornstarch and water, and twice as much sand as cornstarch. In this case, you can use large canfuls or small spoonfuls. Just be sure to use two measures of sand to one measure of cornstarch and one measure of water.

Changing the Proportions

Sometimes you may want to change the proportions of ingredients in the recipe. By changing the proportion of salt to flour, for example, you can change the texture of your dough (see *Experiment with Proportion* on page 46). In this book, soap flakes and water are used to make three different concoctions, just by changing the proportion of flakes to water.

	Soap Flakes	Water
Soap Flake Finger Paint	1/4 cup (50 ml)	1/2 cup (125 ml)
Soap Flake Thick Paint	1 cup (250 ml)	1/2 cup (125 ml)
Soapy Dough	2 cups (500 ml)	1/2 cup (125 ml)

Changing the Ingredients

The first time you mix up a concoction, measure the amounts exactly. Then, if the mixture doesn't suit you, make changes. Is the paint too dull? Add more coloring. Is the dough too crumbly? Add more water. There will be slight variations among different brands of ingredients, so you may need to make minor adjustments. The amount of moisture in the air can also have an effect. Making mixtures on a hot, dry day can bring different results than concocting on a rainy day.

Make changes slowly. Add small spoonfuls a little at a time. It's easy to turn a nice dough into a glop with even a small amount of extra water.

You may want to change the ingredients entirely (see *Experiment with Ingredients* on page 56). Every concoction in this book started out as an experiment. Not every mixture you make will work. Be prepared to try again and again. Keep notes on the ingredients and amounts you use. If your dough is too gloppy, you can look back at your notes and zero in on the right amount of water to use in your next attempt. And when you come up with the greatest, the craziest of all concoctions, you will be able to make it again if you wrote down the ingredients and the amounts as you went along.

Artists are ingenious people who make the most of what they have on hand. What's on *your* shelf or in *your* yard? You may discover that special substance that makes the most mysterious mixture ever concocted!

Happy concocting!

PAINT PIZZAZZ

People have painted for as long as they've had a story to tell. Just as writers use words to share their ideas, painters use images. If you want to know what was important to people at any particular time in history, look at their paintings. Prehistoric people painted hunting scenes on cave walls. Ancient Egyptians painted gods and goddesses, as well as scenes from daily life. Renaissance artists developed techniques to make their paintings look very real, while some of today's artists are more interested in experimenting with color, shape, and texture than in capturing reality in their art.

PAINT CONCOCTIONS

Art Smart

Use a paintbrush to stir pigments and binders together. That way you can immediately test the consistency by painting a stroke on a sheet of scrap paper.

ARTIST'S CHOICE!

Remember, you are the artist in control of the concoction. Feel free to add more binder or pigment to get just the effect you want.

CHARCOAL AND CHICKEN EGGS

Can you believe that charcoal and chicken eggs can be paint ingredients? It's true! All paints are made up of *pigments* (color particles) and *binders* (substances that hold those particles together and help them stick or *adhere*, to the paper, canvas, or wood). The first pigments came from nature: crushed rock, charcoal, ashes, bark, roots, and berries. The first binders also came from nature: animal fats, eggs, and saps. Stone Age artists made their colorful drawings by using a concoction of animal grease and manganese, a brittle metallic substance from the earth. Today pigments and binders also come from metals, petroleum, and artificial materials.

Although paint is available in stores, some artists consider making the paint an important part of the art, just as it was long ago. By experimenting with different concoctions, artists discovered which colors and consistencies worked best. Paint recipes were shared among artists, each one changing the concoction to suit his or her needs.

The paint concoctions in this section use food coloring or tempera powder for the pigments. Kitchen stuff, such as egg yolk, cornstarch, or soap, is used for the binders. Use your concoctions to paint like an ancient Greek and show the beauty of your world. Or, experiment like a modern artist and discover new ways to put paint on paper.

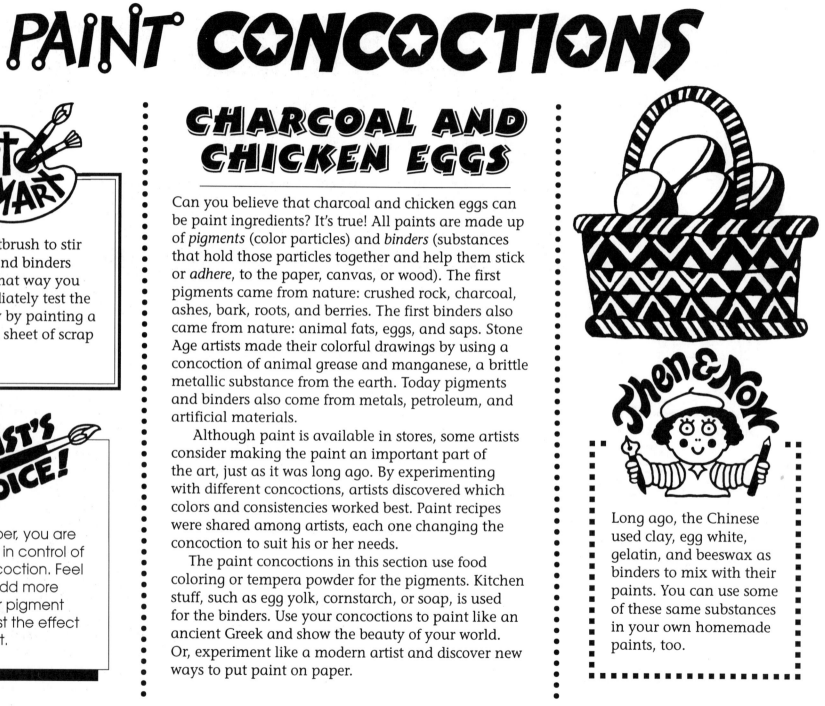

Then & Now

Long ago, the Chinese used clay, egg white, gelatin, and beeswax as binders to mix with their paints. You can use some of these same substances in your own homemade paints, too.

WONDERFUL WATERCOLORS

Watercolors can be used to create many beautiful effects. Five hundred years ago *Albrecht Dürer* used watercolors to paint the details of nature. His tiny, controlled brush strokes formed realistic blades of grass, leaves, and flowers. Fifty years ago *Emil Nolde* watered down his colors so his brush strokes could make bold, flowing flower petals. Watercolors give the artist wonderful choices in artistic expression. Now you can discover these choices for yourself by controlling the amount of water on your brush, the intensity of the color, and the size of your brush.

★ WATERCOLOR CAKES ★

This concoction starts with a magical fizz and ends with a colorful, dried cake. You can make a set of cakes just like the watercolors you buy in a store — but when you make your own you can control the intensity of the color. Your binder will be cornstarch. (Store-bought watercolors are held together with gum arabic from the acacia tree.)

Just swirl a wet brush into the cake, and let the art start!

WHAT YOU NEED

1 tablespoon (15 ml) clear vinegar

1 tablespoon (15 ml) baking soda

1 tablespoon (15 ml) cornstarch

1/2 teaspoon (2 ml) corn syrup

Food coloring

Three small, plastic bottle lids

Small paintbrushes

WHAT YOU DO

1 Mix vinegar and baking soda in a bowl.

2 When the mixture stops fizzing, add cornstarch and corn syrup.

3 Blend together. The mixture will have a strange, cakelike consistency.

4 Divide the mixture among the three lids. For each color, blend in a few drops of food coloring with a paintbrush. (Brighter colors = more food coloring.)

5 Use immediately, or, after the colors have dried into cakes, swirl a wet brush into each color to start painting.

Perhaps the only rule about painting is to *always rinse your brush before dipping into a new color*. Keep a cup of rinse water close by. If you want to mix a new color, use a paint palette or a coated paper plate, but don't mix in the jar or watercolor cake.

Squirrel hair?: Stone Age artists made paintbrushes from feathers, bristles of animal hair, and leaves. Eventually most brushes were made from animal hair, especially the soft, bendable hair of sables and squirrels.

WATERCOLOR TECHNIQUES

Discover the world of wonderful watercolors!

WHAT YOU NEED

Watercolors

Several sizes of brushes

Paper (textured watercolor paper is best)

Cup of rinse water

Experiment with these techniques. Remember to rinse your brush in water before changing colors.

★ Load your brush with paint. Use only the tip to make a very fine line.

★ Watch how the line becomes broader as you press down more firmly.

★ Dab the paint on. Make "paint prints" the size of your brush hairs.

★ Paint two colors side by side. Let their edges flow together on the paper.

What effect does using a wetter brush or wet paper (hold a sheet of paper under running water for a moment) have on the results? The damper the paper, the fuzzier the paint edge. The drier the paper, the sharper the paint edge. Use variations on these techniques to create art that is distinctly yours.

Asian influences: Brush drawing is one of the oldest forms of art still practiced today. The Chinese, Koreans, and Japanese have long been considered brush-drawing masters. In East Asia, artists used very fine brushes, mounted on bamboo handles.

★ SUPER SEE-THROUGH WATERCOLORS ★

WHAT YOU NEED

3 drops of food coloring

1 teaspoon (5 ml) water

Small container

One special quality about watercolors is their *transparency*. That is, you can see through the color to the white paper underneath. This makes the colors seem to glow. Another special quality is the way wet colors fuzz out and flow together. Super See-Through Watercolors maximize the glowing and flowing qualities of watercolors on both paper and cloth (see Batik Banner, page 143 and Playful Parachute, page 146).

WHAT YOU DO

1 Mix the water and food coloring together in the container.

2 See page 9 for how to make this recipe in larger quantities.

★ RAINBOW PAPER ★

Just like a real rainbow, the edges of each color band you paint will fuzz into the next. Watercolors are perfect for painting rainbows and sunsets.

WHAT YOU NEED

Super See-Through Water-colors

Broad paintbrush

Paper (textured watercolor paper is best)

WHAT YOU DO

1 Starting with a wet sheet of paper, paint a band of color across the top of your paper.

2 Rinse your brush and paint the second band touching the first. Let the two colors pool together along their edges.

3 Continue painting bands of color until your entire sheet is colored.

HEY! DON'T FORGET TO RINSE YOUR BRUSH!

ARTIST'S CHOICE!

Let the paper dry completely. Use it as a background for another painting.

— — — — — — — — —

Drip colors on top of the color bands while the paper is still wet. Watch them change color and fuzz out into neat shapes.

CAPTURE A RAINBOW

To see a rainbow, you must have the sun behind you and raindrops falling in front of your eyes. When the rainbow arc's center point, the sun, and your eyes are all in line, the dazzling light show can take place. Sunlight enters a water droplet and breaks apart into an amazing rainbow band of colors called a *spectrum*. The colors always stack up in the same way: red on top, followed by orange, yellow, green, blue, indigo, and violet. (ROY G. BIV: Remember that name and you'll always know the colors of the rainbow, in order.)

To capture a real rainbow on an index card, lean a small mirror against the back edge of a shallow dish of water. Set the dish outside or near a window so that bright sunlight hits the mirror. Hold an index card in front of the mirror. Keep moving it until you can see a spectrum on the card. You just captured a rainbow!

RED
ORANGE
YELLOW
GREEN
BLUE
INDIGO
VIOLET

PICASSO'S WAY

If you think *Pablo Picasso* was a great artist, you are right. But did you also know he was a great inventor? Just like any great inventor, he was never satisfied with the way things were. His inventions were new ways of looking at the world through art.

Picasso taught himself to paint by copying the masterpieces of artists who painted before him. Then, at the age of 25, he went beyond the old painting traditions with his own masterpiece, *The Young Women of Avignon*. He "invented" a new style called *Cubism*. People (and other images, too) were painted from basic shapes such as cubes, cones, and cylinders. No one had ever thought of looking at the world in this way before. Picasso also developed the method of *collage*, which in French means "paste-up" (see page 79), as well as other new artistic styles.

When you decide to "paint a Picasso," don't just paint a great picture; instead, invent a totally new way to look at the world.

★ PAINT GAZING ★

Have you ever gazed at the clouds and thought you were staring at a sky full of ice cream cones, sheep, or sailboats? Well, creating a sheet full of "paint clouds" can be just as much fun!

WHAT YOU NEED

Super See-Through Watercolors (see page 15)

Paintbrushes (several sizes)

Paper (textured watercolor paper is best)

WHAT YOU DO

1 Make random blobs and strokes of watercolor on a sheet of wet paper. Change colors as often as you like.

2 As soon as you have a pleasant collection of "paint clouds," stop. Let the sheet dry.

3 Look at the dry clouds. What do you see? Add details sparingly with a small brush or marker. For example, if a splotch looks like a bird, use sharp lines to paint in the beak and the legs, or outline the wing.

★ FIRST IMPRESSIONS ★

A few strokes of watercolor can create an entire figure. Single paint strokes can become a nose, an arm, or a head of hair. This makes watercolors the perfect paint for creating one-minute impressions of your friends.

WHAT YOU NEED

Watercolors

Paintbrushes (several sizes)

Paper (textured watercolor paper is best)

A timer and a group of friends

WHAT YOU DO

1 Take turns being the model. You can wear crazy clothes, hold a prop, or pose as you are. Now freeze.

2 Set a timer for one minute.

3 Start painting. Don't bother with details. Capture the overall impression of the person with quick paint strokes.

TOULOUSE-LAUTREC'S WAY

Most people go to a cabaret in France to eat, drink, and enjoy a lively show. So did *Toulouse-Lautrec*. But he always brought along his sketch pad. He was famous for capturing life as he found it, and the cabaret, Moulin Rouge, was his favorite place to find it. Quickly, he recorded cancan dancers, singers, and members of the audience. Later these sketches became wonderful oil paintings and lithographs (prints). Look in an art book or encyclopedia for his famous *At the Moulin Rouge*. You can almost hear the lively music and conversation of a Parisian cabaret one hundred years ago! If you enjoyed painting First Impressions, take a small sketch pad and pencil to special places you go. Capture life wherever you find it!

TEMPTING TEMPERAS

Tempera paints are simply paints that can be mixed with water. Tempera works nicely on smooth surfaces such as paper or sealed wood, and it dries quickly. This allows artists to paint one layer of tempera over another without waiting a long time or having the colors mix together on the paper.

★ BASIC TEMPERA ★

This is a rich, all-purpose paint. Use it for any painting project from coloring papier-mache bananas to painting a backyard landscape. The colors are *opaque* which means you can't see through them.

WHAT YOU NEED

1/4 cup (50 ml) powdered tempera

2 tablespoons (25 ml) water

Paintbrush

WHAT YOU DO

1 Mix powdered tempera and water in a jar, until paint is evenly mixed and smooth.

2 Adjust consistency as you like by adding more powder or water.

★ MILK TEMPERA ★

This is similar to Basic Tempera. Simply substitute 2 tablespoons (25 ml) milk for the water in the Basic Tempera concoction. Make only enough for a day or two. Store, just like milk, in the refrigerator.

Milk Tempera is more opaque and somewhat creamier. Mix up a batch of Milk Tempera and Basic Tempera. Test them out by painting different strokes on paper. Which do you prefer?

★ STARCH TEMPERA ★

Starch Tempera applies very smoothly. You can make an interesting textured paint by adding 2 tablespoons (25 ml) of salt to this recipe.

WHAT YOU NEED

2 tablespoons (25 ml) powdered tempera

2 tablespoons (25 ml) liquid starch

Paintbrush

WHAT YOU DO

1 Stir the tempera and starch in a jar, until paint is evenly mixed and smooth.

2 Adjust consistency as you like by adding more powder or starch.

★ PAINT A MURAL ★

Murals are paintings made right on the walls or ceiling of a building. The ancient Egyptians drew murals thousands of years ago that showed how people lived, including people making bread dough and using "saddlestones" to grind the flour.

Why not create a mural of your own that shows how things are done in your house. Place a large piece of butcher paper on newspapers on a washable floor. Then, using tempera paints, paint pictures of people who live in your house, and the types of activities that happen there, too. Try using broad strokes and bold colors to fill up the paper. Invite some friends or family members to join in the mural-making fun.

Then & Now

If given the chance, artists will paint just about anywhere! Over 400 years ago, an artist named *Michelangelo* did many paintings on the ceiling of the Sistine Chapel in Rome, Italy. You can still see these famous paintings today if you visit the chapel.

CONCOCTING COLORS

Every great painter concocts colors. From the three *primary* colors — red, yellow, and blue — many other colors are made. Mix a primary color paint with another primary color paint and you get a *secondary* color paint.

red + yellow = orange

yellow + blue = green

red + blue = purple

Combine a secondary color with a primary color to make turquoise, magenta, chartreuse, and other special colors. Always mix your colors on a palette or coated paper plate — not in the jars!

WHAT YOU NEED

Tempera paints in primary colors

Pencil, paintbrush

Piece of white cardboard

Plastic plate palette

Hole punch, string

★ COLOR STAR ★

See how primary colors combine to make secondary colors by making a color star.

WHAT YOU DO

1 Draw a triangle with all three sides the same length (equilateral triangle) in the center of the cardboard. Draw an upside-down equilateral triangle over the first triangle. Connect the inner points as shown to make six diamonds.

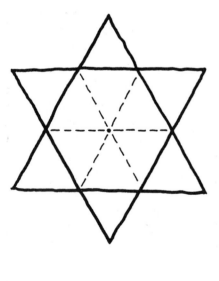

2 Paint a primary color inside every other diamond.

3 Mix yellow and red on the plate. Paint the diamond between the yellow and red diamonds with your concocted orange paint. Continue mixing the other primary colors and painting the secondary colors between them. Be sure to rinse your brush completely each time you dip into a new color.

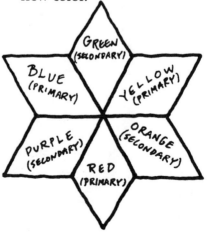

4 Let the star dry. Punch a hole in one of the points, tie a string through it, and hang it near your painting area for reference.

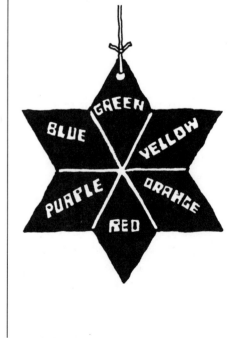

★ BRUSHLESS TEMPERA PAINTING ★

Who says you need a paintbrush! Moving paint around with a marble, string, your breath, and your hand all produce awesome effects. Cover your work surface with newspaper. This can get messy.

★

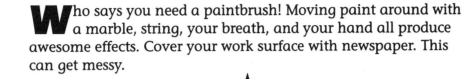

Taking care: Have you ever wondered why many museums don't allow cameras? It's because the flashes of light from cameras can damage paintings. Pollution over many years' time can hurt paintings, too. Leonardo da Vinci's *The Last Supper* was painted during the late 1400s and has been damaged by pollution over the past 500 years. Since 1977, experts have been restoring this famous painting one square inch at a time to remove the dirt, mold, and glue that's built up.

Push a blob: Why not make an "accidental painting"? Put a couple of blobs of different-colored paint in the crease of a piece of paper, refold the paper, and using the palm of your hand, push the paint outward. Open up the paper. Do you see any special pictures in your accidental painting?

★

Drag a string: Fold a piece of paper in half. Unfold it. Dip a piece of string in a small paper plate of paint and place string on paper. Refold the paper with the painted string inside. Press down on the paper as you drag the string side to side and pull it out. Use a new string for each color. Open your painting and enjoy.

Blow it: Thin out some tempera with water. Spoon small puddles of thin paint onto a sheet of paper. Use a straw to blow the puddles in different directions. Watch the paint fan out. Let it dry. Compare the interesting patterns you made with this technique to those from the other techniques.

★

Marble tracks: Cut a sheet of paper to fit in the lid of a box. Set it inside. Place a marble in a small jar of paint. Spoon the paint-covered marble onto the paper. Tilt the lid slowly from top to bottom and side to side. Watch how the marble leaves tracks on the paper. Repeat with as many paint-covered marbles as you like (wash the marble before using it in each color).

Pollock's Way

Hurl paint onto canvas that's on the floor? That's just what Jackson Pollock, an abstract expressionist in the 1940s and '50s, did. He was famous for exploring new ways to get paint onto canvas. He hurled, swirled, dripped, and poured paint on his canvases. Pollock didn't think it mattered how artists put paint on their canvases so long as the painting sent a message to people. What new ways will you discover for putting paint on paper?

★ EGG TEMPERA ★

WHAT YOU NEED

Egg yolk (save egg white for Painting of Egg & Gold, page 25)

Water

Tempera powder

Small paintbrush

Mix up this favorite paint concoction that artists used centuries ago. This opaque paint is great for small, detailed paintings.

WHAT YOU DO

1 Break up the egg yolk in a bowl. Measure 2 teaspoonfuls (10 ml) and put in the jar.

2 Add 1 teaspoon (5 ml) of water. Blend.

3 Add 1 teaspoon (5 ml) of powdered tempera. Stir with the small paintbrush until mixture is smooth.

TRIMMED IN GOLD

More than five centuries ago *Gentile da Fabriano* painted with egg tempera on a wooden panel. His magnificent painting, *Adoration of the Magi*, showed people dressed in fancy clothing and horses with beautiful harnesses in the countryside. To make his painting even more fantastic, da Fabriano added gold metal by hammering thin sheets of gold into the spots he wanted to shine.

A PAINTING OF EGG & GOLD

Paint an egg and gold masterpiece like that of Gentile da Fabriano.

WHAT YOU NEED

Stiff piece of paper

Pencil, small paintbrush, newspaper

Several colors of egg tempera

Egg white

Gold glitter

ARTIST'S CHOICE!

Use egg tempera to paint a design on a hollowed-out egg. Use the egg white to glue on glitter. Nothing is wasted in this art project!

WHAT YOU DO

1 Use a pencil to sketch in a few guidelines for your picture.

2 Mix up your egg tempera, setting aside the egg white.

3 Paint your picture using egg tempera. Let it dry.

4 Paint lines or splotches of egg white where you want the gold to be. Sprinkle the egg white with gold glitter. Let the glitter sit for about 15 minutes. Gently lift the paper over the newspaper to shake off the extra glitter.

★ NOW YOU SEE IT ★

There is something about artists that make them very special — they have very creative minds! They see shapes and forms in the strangest places — a twig on the ground, a piece of sea glass or driftwood on the beach, a rock along a path — and transform them with their imaginations into wondrous things. Let the artist inside you bring a rock to life with your favorite tempera.

WHAT YOU NEED

Smooth, clean rock

Small paintbrush

Several colors of tempera

WHAT YOU DO

1 Take the time to find a very special, smooth rock. It's nice when it fits comfortably in your hand.

2 Clean your rock with soap and water, and dry.

3 Look closely at your rock. Don't think about what you can paint on it. Instead think about what it already looks like. Does it look like a cat curled up for a nap? Maybe it looks like a coiled snake or a baby chick.

4 Think of the outer edge of the rock as the outer edge of your animal. Paint the rock one color. Let it dry. Then paint on details such as eyes, feathers, or a tail.

5 If you like, seal the paint with glue glaze (page 52) or clear acrylic polymer.

ARTIST'S CHOICE!

More than a pet: Your rock can be anything, not just a pet. Maybe it looks like a sailboat, a bunch of grapes, or a car.

– – – – – – – – –

Add-ons: Use white glue to add sequins, yarn, cloth, or other trimmings.

– – – – – – – – –

Behind the scenes: Paint a setting for your rock. Use a piece of tag board about 6" x 6" (15 cm x 15 cm). What would your rock like to sit on? For example, paint a carpet for a napping cat, an ocean for a sailboat, or a vine for a bunch of grapes.

– – – – – – – – –

How about a clothespin?: Upright, it looks like a person. Lay it flat, it might be an alligator. First paint the clothespin one color. Let it dry. Then paint on details giving it a personality. Glue on scrap paper fins or wings, or whatever suits you.

THICK PAINTS

Paintings don't have to be flat. The paint can stick out like on a Van Gogh masterpiece. Spread it on with a butter knife or squeeze it out from a bottle. Use your creative genius and thick paints to create great works of art.

★ SOAP FLAKE PAINT ★

Squeeze or spread this chunky white paint onto paper.

WHAT YOU NEED

1/2 cup (125 ml) soap flakes

1/4 cup (50 ml) water

Eggbeater

WHAT YOU DO

1 Add a small amount of soap flakes to the water; then beat.

2 Continue adding flakes and beating until mixture is evenly blended.

Art Smart

No squeeze bottle? A plastic zip-style sandwich bag works great. Put a glob of thick paint in the corner of the bag. Zip it closed. Make a tiny snip in the corner of the bag where the glob is sitting. Hold the bag in your fist and squeeze. Experiment for a while to get the feel of controlling the paint flow.

ZIP CLOSED

PAINT

TINY SNIP

★ WHITE ON BLACK BOLD ★

Make a bold, white design on heavy, black paper.

WHAT YOU NEED

Heavy sheet of black paper

Soap Flake Paint

Plastic squeeze bottle or zip-style bag

WHAT YOU DO

1 Put soap flake paint in squeeze bottle.

2 Squeeze out interesting white lines of different shapes and thicknesses on black paper. Try solid lines, dotted lines, angles, curves, coils, dots, or dabs. Arrange them in a bold pattern. Hang on your refrigerator or bedroom door.

Make a snowy scene:
Place a glob of paint on dark paper. Use Popsicle stick or your finger to spread the paint into a snowy scene.

- - - - - - - - -

Create abstract art:
Blend food coloring or powdered tempera into the soap flake paint. Make several different colors. Cover a heavy sheet of paper with thick, interesting, different-colored shapes. Don't worry about making your picture look like something. Just enjoy the color and texture of the paint. Use a Popsicle stick or your fingers for spreading.

- - - - - - - - -

Make it stand out:
Use soap flake paint for the main object in your painting. Use basic tempera or watercolors for the background.

VAN GOGH'S WAY

Would you rather have paint or food? *Vincent Van Gogh* chose paint. He was truly a poor, starving artist who could barely afford the paint for his passion. He loved thickly applying paint to the canvas. Some Van Gogh paintings almost look three-dimensional, like sculpture. The brilliant colors stick out over a centimeter from the canvas.

★ DOUGHY PAINT ★

Place doughy paint in a squeeze bottle or zip-style sandwich bag to make thick, puffy lines. Squeeze a design onto cardboard or heavy paper. Doughy paints add a nice finishing touch to papier-mache sculpture. They can be used to outline shapes or add details to a tempera painting, too.

WHAT YOU NEED

1/4 cup (50 ml) flour

1/4 cup (50 ml) salt

1/4 cup (50 ml) water

2 tablespoons (25 ml) tempera powder

Plastic squeeze bottle

WHAT YOU DO

1 Mix all ingredients together until evenly blended.

2 Pour into plastic squeeze bottle or substitute.

★ NAME PLATE ★

Tell the world who you are!

WHAT YOU NEED

3" x 10" (7.5 cm x 25 cm) piece of cardboard

Doughy paints in squeeze bottles

WHAT YOU DO

1 Write your name on the cardboard with doughy paints.

2 Outline the letters with another color of doughy paint. Add as many different colored outlines or tiny details as you wish.

★ SPECIAL STUFF BOX ★

Fill beautifully decorated boxes with special treasures. Give the boxes as gifts or use them to showcase your own special collections.

WHAT YOU NEED

Several colors of Doughy Paint

Special box

Construction paper

Scissors

Paper paste (page 77)

WHAT YOU DO

1 Collect small, nicely shaped cardboard boxes. Candy or jewelry gift boxes work great. Watch for heart-shaped boxes around Valentine's Day.

2 Once you have selected a box, trace the lid onto construction paper. Cut out the paper and paste it to the lid. (If the box is covered with advertising, cover the whole box with paper.)

3 Decorate the lid with a doughy paint design. Remember it can be abstract or a true representation of something. To give your decoration a sparkle, sprinkle on glitter while doughy paint is still wet.

SPECIAL PAINTS

From Bubble Paint to Body Paint, special paints are unique art concoctions you'll love trying again and again. Each time you mix one up, think of new ways to create with these terrific concoctions.

★ ALMOST-OIL SOAP PAINT ★

WHAT YOU NEED

1 tablespoon (15 ml) powdered tempera

1 tablespoon (15 ml) dishwashing soap

Paintbrush

This great concoction has the "feel" of an oil paint. The colors go on smoothly and can be blended together right on the paper.

WHAT YOU DO

Mix powdered tempera and dishwashing soap together until evenly blended.

WHY OIL?

Tempera was the most popular paint until the discovery of oil paint about 500 years ago. Why did artists switch to oils? The chance to change their minds was probably the most important reason. Oil paints use linseed oil as a binder. The linseed oil dries slowly, allowing the artist to blend colors together, right on the canvas. Artists can change things while the paint is still wet. They can even scrape oil paint right off the canvas. How's that for flexibility!

★ PAINT A SELF-PORTRAIT ★

Rembrandt used oils to paint his portrait. Try a self-portrait using Almost-Oil Soap Paint. Like oils, you can blend the soap paint colors together right on the paper.

WHAT YOU NEED

Almost-Oil Soap Paint

Art paper

Paintbrushes (several sizes)

Mirror

WHAT YOU DO

What do you look like? Set up a mirror and look closely at yourself. What is the shape of your head — oval, round, a squarish-jawline? Work slowly and paint every detail. You'll be surprised how much your self-portrait really looks like you.

Rembrandt's Way

Even though there were no cameras in 1650 when Rembrandt lived, we know just what he looked like. He painted pictures of himself — called *self-portraits* — when he was young and old.

We also know what his family looked like. He painted his mother reading the Bible, his son doing homework, and even his pet dog. Rembrandt was famous for capturing the personalities of people. Look at his portraits. If you look beyond the people's old-fashioned clothes, you may think you've seen some of these people before — right in your own neighborhood!

ARTIST'S CHOICE!

Caught in the act: How about catching your family members in the act of being themselves? A good time to paint people is while they are reading, eating, or standing in one place doing a task. You may prefer to do a quick sketch capturing the details you want to remember. Then you can take your time actually doing the painting.

Other ways: Try other mediums for more self-portraits. Use watercolors, temperas, or even thick paints.

Exaggerations: It is fun to exaggerate certain features when you draw a self-portrait, perhaps making your freckles enormous or your smile go from ear to ear. These exaggerated drawings are called *caricatures*. Look in the newspaper for political cartoons, which are often drawn as caricatures.

★ BUBBLE PAINT ★

WHAT YOU NEED

For each color:

2 teaspoons (10 ml) dishwashing liquid

3 tablespoons (40 ml) water

¼ cup (50 ml) powdered tempera

Straw and paper

Newspaper

ARTIST'S CHOICE!

★ Repeat with as many colors as you like.

- - - - - - - -

★ Use the paper to slice through the head of bubbles and capture them on top of the sheet. Let the bubbles burst by themselves.

Have you ever wished you could save a bubble? While you can't keep a bubble from popping, you can save its print before it does. This crazy concoction makes unusual sheets of paper covered with glorious bubble prints. Start blowing!

WHAT YOU DO

1 Mix tempera, water, and dishwashing liquid in a jar. Stir. To brighten the color, add more tempera.

2 Set the jar on newspaper to protect the work surface. Gently blow the straw in the paint mixture. **Absolutely do not suck in.** The mixture tastes horrible and will make you sick! Keep blowing until the bubbles overflow.

3 To capture a bubble print, gently roll a piece of paper on top of the bubbles. They'll leave a print on your paper before they burst.

4 Lay the paper flat to dry.

WHAT'S A BUBBLE?

Bubbles are extremely thin layers of soapy water wrapped around puffs of air. Soap helps water stretch out, so once you have a stretchy film, you can fill it with air by blowing on it — just like bubble gum.

What makes bubbles pop? Holes! Holes happen when something dry, like your hand, touches the fragile film. Even dust can pop a bubble!

AIR PUFF

★ BUBBLES, SWEET BUBBLES ★

By simply adding a little sugar to your soapy water, you can give your bubbles some extra strength. Look carefully in the air after your bubble pops. The sugar also helps you see the deflated soap film.

WHAT YOU NEED

1/4 cup (50 ml) liquid detergent

2 cups (500 ml) water

1 teaspoon (5 ml) sugar

Can opener, can

WHAT YOU DO

1 Mix the ingredients together. Pour the mixture into a pie pan.

2 Have a grown-up help you cut both ends out from a can. Take care not to cut yourself.

3 Dip one end in the mixture. Blow into the other end (but don't put your mouth on it) for big, beautiful bubbles.

★ MARBLED MIXTURE ★

Use this concoction to make paper look as beautiful as marble stone. Swirl the floating colors; then capture their pattern on paper. This paper is wonderful to use to frame pictures, cover books, use as stationery, or any number of things.

WHAT YOU NEED

For each color:

1 tablespoon (15 ml) acrylic paint

2 tablespoons (25 ml) water

½ cup (125 ml) liquid starch

Cookie sheet, roasting pan, or tray

Paintbrush or comb

WHAT YOU DO

1 For each color, blend acrylic paint and water. Set aside.

2 Fill the pan with the liquid starch. Use a paintbrush to drop paint mixture onto the starch. To avoid a muddy look, use only two or three colors at a time.

3 Use a comb or paintbrush to gently swirl the colors.

4 Lay a sheet of paper on top of the colors.

5 Carefully lift the paper. The swirls of color will now be on the paper. Set paper aside to dry.

6 Add more paint and repeat these steps to make more marbled paper.

ARTIST'S CHOICE!

Lay the face of a white paper bag in the mixture for a beautiful gift bag.

– – – – – – – –

Lay the face of a white envelope in the mixture for unusual stationery.

– – – – – – – –

Lay an index card into the mixture to make a postcard or bookmark.

Art Smart

Make a marble rake: Tape toothpicks onto a ruler. Space them evenly, about 1 inch (2.5 cm) apart. Drag your rake through the colors to make interesting patterns. Raked patterns are more regular than random swirls.

IT'S NO MIX UP

Why does oily paint float on top of the water? It's because oil and water have different densities. *Density* is determined by how heavy something is compared with its size, or *volume*. If you have a small kitchen scale, weigh a spoonful of oil and a spoonful of water. You'll discover that the water weighs more than the oil. Equal amounts of the liquids don't have the same weight. That's why oil can float on top of water.

Where in the world can you see this happening? Well, on a rainy day, notice how oil from cars and trucks floats on top of rain puddles. Or, before you shake up the salad dressing, notice how the vegetable oil floats on top of the vinegar. Why do you think wildlife suffers so much when an oil spill happens? A thick layer of petroleum oil floats on top of the ocean, coating swimming birds and animals at the same time.

Nature's art: Sculptors have made monuments, sculptures, and buildings from marble stone for hundreds of years. And it's no wonder — after all, marble has beautiful swirls of color made entirely by nature. These swirls form when a mixture of small rock pieces (limestone and dolomite) melt and harden, over and over again (called *recrystallizing*). This melting and hardening happens, in part, because of enormous changes in the heat and pressure beneath the earth's surface.

★ BODY PAINT ★

Paint your nose! Paint your toes! These paints are easy to make, use, and remove.

WHAT YOU NEED

6 teaspoons (30 ml) cornstarch

3 teaspoons (15 ml) cold cream

3 teaspoons (15 ml) water

Food coloring

Muffin tin or 6 film canisters

Small paintbrushes

WHAT YOU DO

1 For each color, mix: 1 teaspoon (5 ml) cornstarch, 1/2 teaspoon (2 ml) cold cream, and 1/2 teaspoon (2 ml) water. Mix each color in its own film canister or muffin tin cup.

2 Add a few drops of food coloring. Stir until well blended.

Tattoos: Paint a small picture on your friend's cheek or on your own arm. Try animals, basic shapes, thunderbolts, sun, moon, rainbow, flowers.

Masks: Instead of drawing a small zebra tattoo on your cheek, you become the zebra! Paint stripes across your face. Give yourself an animal nose, eyes, and mouth. Try making animals, superheroes and superheroines, monsters, clowns, or any creature.

Wearables: Paint a necklace around your neck, a wristwatch on your arm, or elf shoes on your feet.

Hand puppets: Make a fist. See how your tucked-in thumb looks like the lower jaw of a face? Paint your hand to look like a creature. You can also make finger puppets by giving each finger a special painted personality.

Clown faces: Bold face paint helps the audience see a clown's expression, even from faraway. Each clown has his or her own special face design called a *working face*. Design your own clown working face — either happy or sad, depending on how you feel and what you want to communicate.

SCARY STUFF

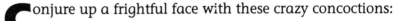

Conjure up a frightful face with these crazy concoctions:

Blood = Corn syrup + red food coloring

Warts = Corn syrup + puffed cereal

Beard = Corn syrup + coffee grounds

White hair = Flour. Rub a small amount all over your head.

Creepy skin = Unflavored gelatin + water. Add food coloring or use plain. Rub globs on your face.

KID BIZ

Your artistic skills are perfected. You've concocted the greatest body paints. Why not set up a body painting booth at the next fair in your school, church, or synagogue? You can help raise money for a charity and have fun, too. Call the fair organizers for rules and regulations. Or, set yourself up on your front lawn on a summer's day and decorate the neighborhood kids.

WHAT YOU NEED

Two chairs or stools (one for you and one for your customer)

A small table for setting up your paints

A mirror for the customer to admire the results

A poster displaying the tattoos you paint best

Photographs of a few friends wearing your face paintings

A money box filled with some change

WHAT YOU DO

On a hot day, set up under a tree or have a grown-up help you set up a beach umbrella. You want your customers to be comfortable. Be sure to charge more for designs that take a long time or use a lot of paint. You may also want to sell canisters of your crazy concoction colors. Give them special names such as *Terrific Turquoise* or *Raspberry Red*. You're in business!

TATTOOS 10¢ EACH

Then & Now

Where in the world?: Imagine covering your face with pig grease and red powder. Next you paint on a pattern of bold dots. That's exactly what women do in Papua, New Guinea to look attractive.

People have painted designs on their bodies for thousands of years, and for different reasons. Some tribe members painted themselves to look like the animals they hunted, believing this made them powerful hunters. Others wore special paintings for festivals. Today, women of India paint beautiful lacelike designs on their hands for their wedding day.

FABULOUS FINGER PAINTS

If concoctions mean ushy, gushy, and mushy fun to you, then this is where you want to be. These four fabulous concoctions each have a different look and feel. Powdered tempera or food coloring are the pigments. Pick a binder you already have on your kitchen shelf — cornstarch, flour, soap flakes, or liquid starch — and let those fingers start painting!

THE GROUND RULES

Finger painting can be a mess, but what a marvelous mess. Follow these rules and grown-ups will say yes when you ask to finger paint again.

★ Work outdoors if possible.

★ Cover your work surface with plenty of newspaper.

★ Wear old clothes or a smock.

★ Keep a bucket of soapy water and an old towel nearby for washing hands.

★ Keep sponges handy. Clean up before spilled paint dries.

★ Work on slick paper, heavy enough to withstand the friction of your fingers, so it won't tear.

FOR BIG KIDS, TOO!

Don't just let the little kids have all the fun. Get in there and feel that paint! Think of finger painting as *moving globs of paint across the paper* with all parts of your hands, until you see something you like. Try some of these methods.

★ Use the side of your hand to cut through the paint and leave strokes of white paper showing.

★ Push the heel of your hand into the paint to leave white splotches.

★ Use your entire forearm for huge bold strokes.

★ Try one, two, or three fingers at a time.

★ Use fingernails for details.

★ Feet, toes, knuckles, elbows? If you are painting outdoors, why not?

Think of your own ways to move the paint around. It's fun to just experiment. You may see a familiar shape in the strokes you make. Maybe it looks like the petal of a flower or a mountain peak. Go ahead and try to make an entire scene. You'll be amazed at how realistic you can make a finger painting.

★ STARCH FINGER PAINT ★

WHAT YOU NEED

2 tablespoons (25 ml) liquid starch

1 tablespoon (15 ml) powdered tempera

WHAT YOU DO

1 Put starch and tempera in a bowl. Use a separate bowl for each color.

2 Mix until evenly blended.

or

1 Pour starch onto finger-paint paper.

2 Sprinkle powdered tempera on top.

3 Mix as you paint.

★ CORNSTARCH FINGER PAINT ★

WHAT YOU NEED

1/4 cup (50 ml) cornstarch

3/4 cup (175 ml) water

Food coloring or powdered tempera dissolved in a little water

WHAT YOU DO

1 Combine cornstarch with a little of the water in a pot. Stir until they form a smooth paste. Now stir in the rest of the water.

2 Have a grown-up help you stir over low heat. Don't let the mixture stick to the pot.

3 Simmer until clear and thick. Cool.

4 Divide into bowls and blend in coloring. Or, blend in the color as you finger paint.

ARTIST'S CHOICE!

Add sand or salt for texture.

- - - - - - - - - - - - -

Add fragrance, food extracts, or spices.

- - - - - - - - - - - - -

Try finger painting with edible stuff: whipped dessert toppings, pudding, or canned cake frosting. Sprinkle dry dessert gelatin on wet paper.

- - - - - - - - - - - - -

Try dragging or dabbing these tools in the paint: sponge, comb, brush, potato masher, fork, or crumpled waxed paper.

- - - - - - - - - - - - -

Tape one, long, continuous sheet of paper to a tabletop or along the sidewalk. Gather your friends and let everyone finger paint at once.

- - - - - - - - - - - - -

Finger paint in a plastic tray. When you like your design, place a sheet of paper on top of it. Rub the back of the paper with your dry hands. Slowly lift up the paper. You'll make a finger-paint print!

MUNCH'S WAY

Edvard Munch, a Norwegian artist who painted in the late 1800s and early 1900s, often used long, wavy lines to express emotion, movement, and even sound in his paintings. He made smeared-looking images that created strong reactions from those who observed them. One of his most famous paintings is called *The Scream*. You can almost hear the sound as you look at the painting.

Although Munch didn't use finger paints, finger painting is a wonderful way for you to experience Munch's painting style. Create a picture using wavy lines bordered by more wavy lines — like ripples in the water — with your fingers. You may even wish to close your eyes and imagine as you paint!

★ FLOUR FINGER PAINT ★

WHAT YOU NEED

1/2 cup (125 ml) flour

1/2 cup (125 ml) water

1 tablespoon (15 ml) liquid detergent

Food coloring or powdered tempera

WHAT YOU DO

1 Combine flour, detergent, and water in the mixing bowl. Stir until they form a smooth paste.

2 Divide into bowls and blend in coloring. Or, blend in the color as you finger paint.

★ SOAP FLAKE FINGER PAINT ★

WHAT YOU NEED

1/4 cup (50 ml) soap flakes

1/2 cup (125 ml) warm water

Food coloring

Eggbeater

WHAT YOU DO

1 Add a small amount of soap flakes to water in bowl; then beat.

2 Continue adding and beating until mixture looks like whipped cream.

3 Divide into bowls and blend in coloring. Or, blend in the color as you finger paint.

ARTIST'S CHOICE!

For some good, clean fun, whip up a batch of Soap Flake Finger Paint before your next bath. Finger paint the bathtub walls.

- - - - - - - - - -

Use white Soap Flake Finger Paint on dark-colored paper.

★ MYSTERY TRACKS ★

Help! It's after me! Use your hand to create the footprint of a strange beast. Then print mysterious tracks across the paper.

WHAT YOU NEED

Finger paint (Temperas also work well. See pages 19–26.)

Hand-sized tray or large paper plate

Art paper

WHAT YOU DO

1 Place finger paint in a tray large enough to put your hand in easily.

2 Imagine a strange beast. Think about what its foot looks like and the print it would leave. Experiment using different parts of your hand to make a weird footprint, hoof print, or paw print.

3 Once you are satisfied with the print, make a mirror copy with your other hand.

4 Decide if your creature has two, four, or an unusual number of legs! Think about how it would travel and what sort of tracks it would leave. Make those tracks across the paper.

Footprint ideas: Try to copy the tracks of real animals. Look for a book at the library that shows animal tracks.

★ Use your fingertips for short toe prints. Print your entire fingers for long toe prints. How many toes does your beast have?

★ The curved edge of your hand makes claw shapes or the edge of a hoof.

★ Try different pad shapes. A tight fist makes a round shape. An open fist makes a long shape. Tightly stretch your fingers to keep them out of the paint. Print only your palm for a broad-shaped pad.

★ Combine toe print and pad prints into an interesting footprint.

Make unusual wrapping paper by covering the sheet with tracks going every which way.

- - - - - - - - - -

Have several strange beasts trek across the paper. Make the prints different colors.

- - - - - - - - - -

Now that you know all the shapes your hand can make, print other patterns with parts of your hand such as prints of flowers, people, creatures, and interesting shapes. Then repeat them all over the paper.

HANDS-ON DOUGHS

Dough art is hundreds of years old. It may have been started by South American Indians. Perhaps it began when someone, like you, accidentally discovered how moldable and hard-drying dough could be. Because artists are ingenious people who can create with whatever materials they have at hand, recipes were shared and passed on from artist to artist, each changing the recipe to suit the needs of the particular project.

Try the concoctions in this section as they are written. Then experiment and change the ingredients to suit your artistic style and needs. Get to know the different concoctions and how they feel in your hands.

★ NO-COOK FLOUR DOUGH ★

Dough wise: Each dough concoction has a feel all its own — one that you can best discover by making the dough and working with it in your hands. Some of these dough concoctions will seem best suited to making a large sculpture, while another concoction may feel most suitable for a fragile ornament, a three-dimensional picture, or a funky piece of jewelry. Never underestimate the power of dough. A humble glob of dough can be transformed into a noble queen puppet, fabulous jewelry as nice as you can buy in any craft shop, or even a back-to-the-future fossil. All it takes is a little creative inspiration and some basic dough-wise skills.

No cooking means you can make this simple dough without grown-up help and begin creating instantly! The more you knead, the better the dough gets.

WHAT YOU NEED

2 cups (500 ml) flour

1 cup (250 ml) salt

1 cup (250 ml) water

WHAT YOU DO

1 Combine flour and salt in a bowl. Stir.

2 Add water and mix thoroughly.

3 Gather the mixture in your hands. Press it into a firm ball.

4 Put the ball on a clean surface and knead until you have a smooth dough.

EXPERIMENT WITH PROPORTION

Proportion is the relationship of the amount of one ingredient to another. Instant flour dough is made from flour, salt, and water. But in what amounts? You can have flour make up four-fifths of the concoction for a stiff dough or only half of the concoction for a softer dough. You be the master dough-maker. Use this chart as a guide for varying the proportion of flour to salt. Which proportion do you think makes the best dough?

Flour	Salt	Water
4 cups (1 l)	1 cup (250 ml)	1 1/2 cups (375 ml)
3 cups (750 ml)	1 cup (250 ml)	1 1/3 cups (325 ml)
2 cups (500 ml)	1 cup (250 ml)	1 cup (250 ml)
1 cup (250 ml)	1 cup (250 ml)	2/3 cup (150 ml)

★ COOKED FLOUR DOUGH ★

Ah, the wonderful feeling of warm dough! Start molding as soon as it has cooled just enough to handle comfortably. This dough is nice and elastic. It's crumble-free and the oil makes it slow drying, allowing you plenty of time to work and rework your creation.

WHAT YOU NEED

2 cups (500 ml) flour

1 cup (250 ml) salt

2 cups (500 ml) water

2 tablespoons (25 ml) oil

1 tablespoon (15 ml) cream of tartar

WHAT YOU DO

1 Combine all ingredients in a pot.

2 Ask a grown-up to help you stir over low heat. Don't let the mixture stick to the pot. Keep stirring and cooking until the mixture looks like mashed potatoes — instead of like soup.

3 Remove pot from the stove and cool until ready to handle. Gather the mixture together with the spoon.

4 Put the glob on a floured surface and knead until you have a smooth dough.

Do you knead your dough? Please do! Kneading is the most important part of working the dough. Start with a dough glob on your work surface. Push it down with the heels of your hands. Fold the dough over and push it down again. Do this again and again until the dough feels smooth and elastic.

What's happening? Kneading releases the *gluten* which is a protein in the flour. Gluten forms the "glue" or structure of the dough, making it stretchable and nice to work with. So your dough will be much happier if it's needed — I mean kneaded!

ARTIST'S CHOICE!

Feel free to knead more flour into the dough if it's too sticky. Add a little more water if the dough is too crumbly. Keep flour in a shaker and water in a spray bottle nearby as you work.

- - - - - - - - -

Make dough glue, called *slip*, by dissolving a small piece of dough in some water. Rub slip in places you want pieces of dough to stick to each other.

- - - - - - - - -

To prevent drying, cover dough that sits out as you work with a damp towel.

- - - - - - - - -

Keep dough fresh longer by adding a few drops of mouthwash. Store in airtight container in the refrigerator.

TOOLS OF THE TRADE

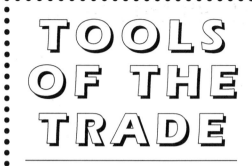

Don't worry if you don't have this exact list. Feel free to improvise.

Wooden board. While you can work directly on a table, it's nice to have a wooden board to work on for easy clean up.

Small, flat board. Use this to give a hunk of dough flat sides.

Two narrow boards. These give slabs straight edges.

Dull knife. Dough is so soft, a dull table knife or nail file works fine. Use it to cut dough. A dull knife or spatula is also useful for scraping up a piece of dough stuck to the work surface.

Rolling pin. Use to flatten dough.

Pencil. Use as a mini rolling pin. Use point to make dotted textures or lines.

Cookie cutters or open-ended cans. Useful for making basic flat shapes.

Toothpick, ice cream stick, open paper clip, drinking straw, nail. Use for details such as dots, lines, and other indentations. Use to make holes in beads or holes for hanging pieces.

Screen, mesh, lace. Press into the dough for texture.

Embossed end of a spoon, bolts, shells, macaroni, buttons, spools, kitchen gadgets. Press into the dough for texture and design.

Garlic press. Makes a mass of noodles or hair.

Fork, toothbrush, or comb. Drag along or press into surface for texture.

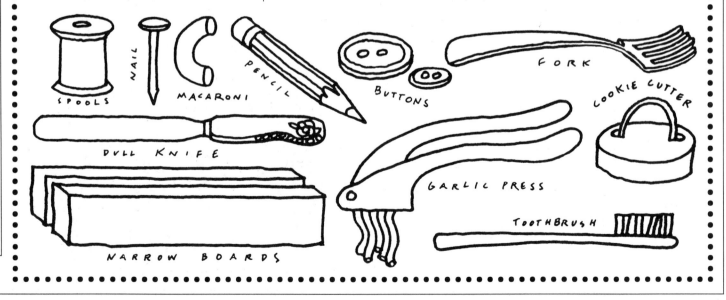

SPOOLS · NAIL · MACARONI · PENCIL · BUTTONS · FORK · COOKIE CUTTER · DULL KNIFE · GARLIC PRESS · TOOTHBRUSH · NARROW BOARDS

★ DOUGH SCULPTURE ★

What can you make with dough? A better question is what can't you make! In fact the more unlikely the item you choose, the more imaginative your sculpture often turns out to be. Take a look around you for ideas. Are you outside? How about sculpting trees, an insect, a car, a bird. Are you inside? Try sculpting the sofa, the television, a plate of fruit, the cat. Feeling silly? Try sculpting odd shapes or place an elephant in a tree!

WHAT YOU NEED

Flour dough

WHAT YOU DO

Once you've chosen the subject, inspect it carefully and decide what basic shapes to make. Use tools to add details and special effects. The more details you add, the more realistic your sculpture will appear.

Use your creative genius to make anything you want in your own way. Here are some ideas to get you started:

People. Babies, grandparents, people with interesting costumes or uniforms such as ballerinas, firefighters, or clowns; people with props such as musical instruments, tools, or seated on furniture. Try sitting, standing, or action poses.

Creatures. Monsters, mammals, lizards, fish, insects, birds, dinosaurs, aliens. Try sleeping, sitting, and standing poses.

Household items. Kitchen items, foods, furniture, hardware.

Vehicles. Buses, trucks, boats, cars, planes, rockets, trains.

Abstract shapes. Any interesting shape, textured or decorated in any way you please.

ARTIST'S CHOICE!

Colored dough. Knead in food coloring or add to the water before mixing.

- - - - - - -

Fragrant dough. Knead in cinnamon, vanilla, peppermint, or other flavorings. Add a few drops of cologne.

- - - - - - -

Sparkling dough. Knead in glitter.

- - - - - - -

Marbleized dough. Knead the color only partly throughout the dough. You can also knead two different-colored balls of dough together. Stop kneading when you like the way the colors are marbleized.

MOLDING TECHNIQUES

Use these basic molding techniques to make the following sculpting shapes. Use the ideas to make most anything you can imagine!

Ball. Roll a hunk of dough between the palms of your hands in a circular motion.

Egg. Start with a ball. Roll it back and forth between your palms until it becomes oval instead of round. Use your fingers to finish off the egg-shaped ends.

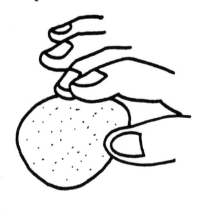

Drop. Pinch one end of the ball with your fingers. Make the dough look like a giant raindrop.

Snake. Roll a hunk of dough back and forth between your palms until it becomes long and thin. Control the thickness by continuing to roll it back and forth on a board. Wet your hands if the snake starts to crack.

Cylinder. Form a fat snake. Now cut off the ends.

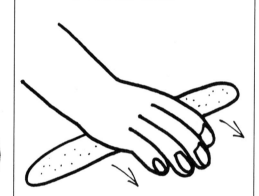

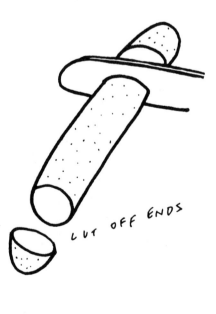

CUT OFF ENDS

Cube. Form a cylinder. Now take a small, smooth, flat board and press it on top of a rounded side of the cylinder. The sides that were against the board and the work surface should be flat. Turn so one rounded side is facing up, and repeat pressing with board, until all sides are flat. You should now have a cube with six flat sides.

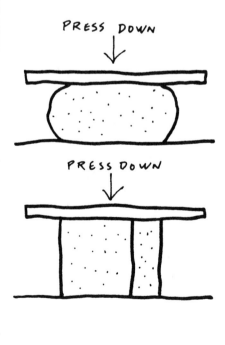

PRESS DOWN

PRESS DOWN

Slabs. Set a ball of dough on the work surface between two boards. Use the rolling pin to roll the dough between them. The slab will have two straight edges. You can cut the other two edges straight with a dull knife.

Flat shapes. Any shape can be flattened. Flatten a small ball between your thumb and forefinger to make a pancake. Use a rolling pin to flatten a snake into a ribbon. Press larger shapes between a board and the work surface.

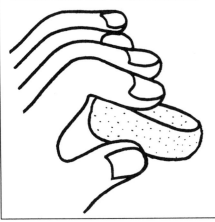

SPECIAL EFFECTS

Candy stripes. Twist two different-colored snakes together.

Stripes. Stack thin cylinders of different colors. Press.

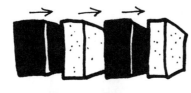

Rainbow. Stack several different-colored slabs on top of each other. Cut through the slabs to make rainbows.

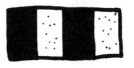

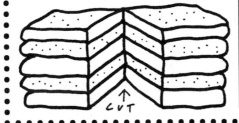

Jelly roll. Set a slab on top of a different-colored slab. Roll them up together. Slice the roll to make pinwheel pancakes.

Multi-colored pancakes. Press three or more colors of snakes together. Gently roll them into one fat snake. Slice into multi-colored pancakes. You can also surround the colored snakes with a slab of color. This will give the multi-colored pancakes a nice border.

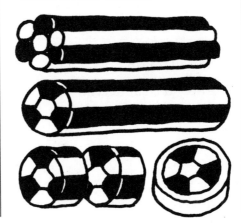

Ears or petals. Pinch one side of a pancake or flattened drop.

PINCH

Scales, feathers, or roof shingles. Layer rows of pancakes or flattened drops.

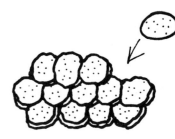

Polka dots and other patterns. Press small pieces of colored clay into clay of another color.

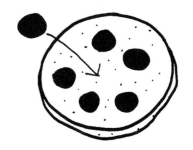

DRYING DOUGH

Let dough pieces dry in a warm, dry place. This can take several days. Dough can also be baked. Ask a grown-up to set the oven on low, about 300°F (150°C). Place your creations on a cookie sheet. Check the pieces about every half hour. Thick, chunky pieces will take longer than small, thin pieces.

COLORING AND FINISHING DOUGH

If you work with colored doughs, there is no need to paint your creation. If you use natural-colored dough, you may wish to paint it after it's dry. When painting or glazing, please be certain you are in a well-ventilated room, or work outdoors. You can use:

★ Tempera paint (see page 19)

★ Felt-tip markers

★ Acrylic paint

Here's how to "glaze" the dough, or seal it and give it a shiny surface:

★ Paint with glue glaze, a mixture of equal parts white glue and water.

★ Paint small art works with clear nail polish.

★ Apply a clear acrylic sealer with grown-up help.

Michelangelo's Way

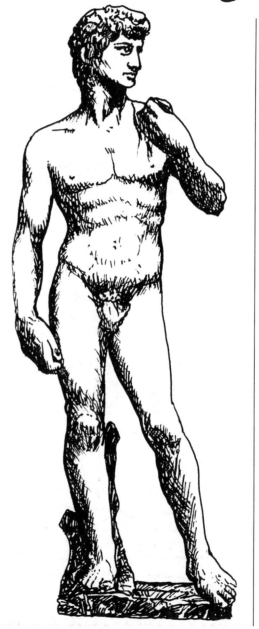

Michelangelo was a genius with a great love for sculpture. He thought of the marble he carved as a prison holding a sculpture inside. It was his job to free the imagined trapped figures from the block by chiseling them out. He picked out his own blocks of marble from the quarry, looking at each one for a figure-to-be.

His 18-foot statue of David was a masterpiece. First he chose a piece of marble no one else wanted. (Other sculptors thought the marble was too long and flat.) Michelangelo probably planned the figure of David from sketches and small models of clay or wax. Next he chiseled to free one arm, then the other, then the entire, huge body from the stone. Michelangelo left a little bit of stone uncarved at the top of David's head to show everyone how perfectly he had calculated the height.

★ SMALL WORLDS ★

Group several sculptures together in an interesting setting. Ordinary or extraordinary, any setting can make a funny, fascinating, or fabulous sculpture scene.

WHAT YOU NEED

Flour dough

Stiff piece of cardboard

White glue

WHAT YOU DO

Use the cardboard as a base. Group sculptures that go together into a scene. For example, make a castle and add a knight, a horse, and a dragon for a medieval scene. Or, set a sculpture of your dad on a sculpture of a sofa. Give him some books to read. Add a reading lamp and a TV. Maybe your dog is napping on a rug next to him. Want to make your sculpture weird? Replace the sculpture of your dad with one of a dragon. Let the dragon sit on the sofa and watch TV. When you are satisfied with your arrangement, glue the pieces in place.

HOLD THE MAYO

For centuries artists sculpted images of people, gods, or animals. Now look what 20th century artists are sculpting! Visit New York's Museum of Modern Art to see Claes Oldenburg's *Cheeseburgers with Everything*, or Robert Hudson's *Fat Knat*. What sculpture might you be dreaming up for the 21st century?

★ SCULPT-A-PICTURE ★

Create a picture that seems to come alive, because it's rising right out of the background! Make a scene from nature, your life, a portrait, or a free-form design.

WHAT YOU NEED

Flour dough

Stiff piece of cardboard (about 5" x 7" or 12.5 cm x 17.5 cm)

ARTIST'S CHOICE!

Roll out snakes in several colors. Use them to write words. Decorate the words with tiny creatures, objects, or other decorations.

- - - - - - - -

Write and decorate your name to make a special name plate for your room.

WHAT YOU DO

1 For the background, roll out a thin layer of dough on the cardboard. (Dampen the cardboard if the dough won't stick.) Keep in mind that this is a three-dimensional picture to be hung, so this is the background — not the base.

2 Plan the picture by sketching the basic shapes with a toothpick. Or, decide where shapes will be as you go.

3 Press flattened shapes into the dough layer. "Mistakes" can simply be lifted off. Wet the bottom side of the shape if you are having trouble getting it to stick (see how to make slip, page 48). You can stick on a dog and then stick on a tail that even protrudes further off the background.

4 Don't forget to add texture using your tools.

WHEN IS A SCULPTURE NOT A SCULPTURE?

Not all sculpture stands on its own. Sometimes raised images are sculpted right out of a picture. This art form is called *bas-relief.* Ancient people used bas-relief to retell great events. Figures jut out of the background, making the picture seem more real and exciting. How about making a bas-relief of a great event in your life? Just follow the Sculpt-a-Picture directions.

★ CORNSTARCH DOUGH ★

This dough is very soft in texture and white in color. It is especially well suited for making ornaments and jewelry.

WHAT YOU NEED

1 cup (250 ml) cornstarch

2 cups (500 ml) baking soda

1 1/4 cups (300 ml) water

WHAT YOU DO

1 Combine all ingredients in a pot.

2 Ask a grown-up to help you stir over low heat. Don't let the mixture stick to the pot. Keep stirring and cooking until the mixture looks like mashed potatoes — instead of like soup.

3 Remove pot from the stove, cool slightly, and gather the mixture together with a spoon.

4 Put the glob on a floured surface and when cool enough to handle, knead until you have a smooth dough.

EXPERIMENT WITH INGREDIENTS

On page 46, you varied the proportion of the ingredients. Now try varying just one of the ingredients. Stick with one cup (250 ml) of cornstarch and one cup (250 ml) of water. Follow all the same steps as for the original Cornstarch Dough recipe, but this time leave out the baking soda. Instead add either salt or flour as shown in the chart below.

Cornstarch	Special Ingredient	Water
1 cup (250 ml)	2 cups (500 ml) salt	1 cup (250 ml)
1 cup (250 ml)	1 cup (250 ml) flour	1 cup (250 ml)

Compare the different doughs. Which is soft? stiff? crumbly? elastic? For which can you easily find the ingredients on your kitchen shelf? Which dough feels best to you?

Art Smart

★ Cornstarch blends best with cold liquid. So, to avoid cornstarch lumps, blend with twice as much water as cornstarch before cooking. Then cook this mixture with the remaining water called for in the recipe.

★ If dough is too hot to handle when it first comes out of the pot, cover it with a damp cloth while you wait for it to cool.

WHAT THICKENS GRAVY AND RELIEVES DIAPER RASH?

Cornstarch! It's one of the oldest packaged foods in America. Cornstarch comes from the *endosperm* part of a corn kernel. It's most often used to thicken foods such as pudding. As you may have noticed, cornstarch has a glossy appearance when cooked. This makes it an ideal ingredient for attractive gravies and even finger paints (see page 41). It's also useful for absorbing moisture.

What else can you do with cornstarch?

★ Dust it in the inside of your tennis shoes to absorb moisture.

★ Use as an after-bath dusting powder.

★ Make an itch-relieving paste by blending some with water.

★ Sprinkle on stains to absorb the grease before laundering.

★ And for the most fun of all, use in dough, paste, and paint concoctions!

★ MONSTER MAGNETS ★

Transform your refrigerator door into a spooky place where monsters lurk!

WHAT YOU NEED

Cornstarch dough

Tempera (page 19) or acrylic paint

Glue glaze (page 52) or clear acrylic sealer

White glue (or hot glue with grown-up help)

Magnet

WHAT YOU DO

1 Roll out dough to about 1/4 inch (5 mm) thick.

2 Do you want to make a monster head or the entire body? Use cookie cutters or the open end of a can to cut a base shape from the dough. You can also cut your own free-form shape with a dull knife.

3 Roll some snake pieces. Use these for eyelids, noses, arms, fins, or wherever you want to build up dough.

4 See Tools of the Trade on page 48 for ways to texture your monster. Remember that a garlic press makes great hair. Fork holes make prickly skin or fur.

5 Once you're satisfied that you've made your monster as creepy as possible, let it dry thoroughly. Then follow directions on page 52 for decorating and glazing. Be sure the front, sides, and back of the monster are completely sealed.

6 Use white glue or hot glue with grown-up help to attach a magnet to the back. Display with fear on a metal surface.

ARTIST'S CHOICE!

Use a straw or nail to make a hole at the top of the monster before it dries. Hang monsters around the house with ribbon, yarn, or string.

- - - - - - - -

Anything or anyone can become a magnet. Make something as ordinary as a bunch or grapes or as outrageous as an alien. Planet earth, your cat, or a howling coyote are possible magnet ideas, too.

CUT OUT SHAPE WITH COOKIE CUTTER OR DULL KNIFE

ATTACH MAGNET TO BACK

★ JAZZY JEWELRY ★

WHAT YOU NEED

Cornstarch dough

String

Toothpick

Tempera (page 19) or acrylic paint

Glue glaze (page 52) or clear acrylic sealer

Any shape of bead or pendant can be made with cornstarch dough or with bread dough (see page 63). Just remember to poke a stringing hole through your creations before they dry. String them on something special — a piece of gimp, leather, waxed linen, or satin cord. Or, use a piece of natural-dyed cotton string. You decide!

WHAT YOU DO

1 Make any or all of the shapes as described in Molding Techniques on page 50. Remember to put in the hole for threading with a toothpick. (A good way to check the stringing hole is to look through and make sure you can see light.)

2 Then, make a pendant for the center of the necklace.

★ Roll the dough flat.

★ Use a knife or your fingers to make a special shape. You might make a star, sun, face, or animal. Keep it simple.

★ Make the hole through the sides of the pendant so that the pendant will lay flat on your chest. Or, make two side-by-side holes to lace the pendant string through.

3 Decorate the beads by either leaving them in their natural color; using pre-colored dough to make beads; or make colorful pancake, marbleized, candy stripe, or polka dot beads (see Special Effects on page 51). Draw patterns on beads using a toothpick, if you wish.

4 Color and finish dried beads (see Coloring and Finishing Dough, page 52).

5 Start stringing! Lay out beads in the order you want them on your necklace. Start planning from the center and move outward, placing your pendant bead in the center. Then place the same kinds of bead on either side of the pendant, to give your necklace balance.

Make a pin, barrette, or earrings: Purchase backings for these items at a craft or bead shop, or collect them from old jewelry that no one wants anymore (ask permission first). Plan the size and shape of the piece to fit the jewelry backing. Set the backings into dough before it dries. Or, glue into place after dough is dry.

Bead it!: Ever since prehistoric times, people have greatly valued beads. Because they were easy to transport and often made from precious substances, beads were convenient for trade. When Europeans first brought glass beads to America, a single bead could be traded for an entire beaver fur!

People have used beads for centuries to adorn their bodies. The neck, wrist, ankle, or waist are all places to add bead ornaments. Beads are also sewn onto clothing. The Huichol Indians of Mexico even decorate the ears of their pets with beads for protection.

What are beads made from? The list is long. Porcupine quills, coral, shells, bone, crystal, gold-coated clay, and even plastic are among the many materials often used. And beads come in all shapes. The Chorotegan Indians of Costa Rica made thin disk beads of green jadeite, while the turquoise heishi beads of southwest North America are among the smallest beads known.

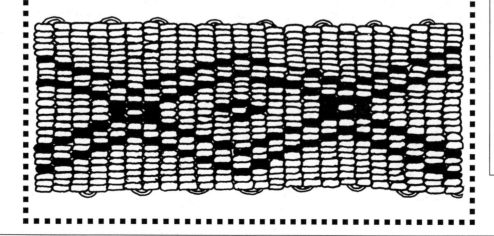

How about making one of these theme necklaces:

★ **A celestial necklace.** Make a moon or sun pendant bead for the center. On either side, string a pattern of several ball beads followed by a star bead.

★ **A food necklace.** Make tiny food beads such as ice cream cones, hot dogs, apples, or bananas. Put these special beads between several ball or tube beads.

★ **A nature necklace.** Make simple wildlife-shaped beads such as fish, butterflies, flowers, or leaves. Make a large one for the center bead. Make smaller ones to alternate with simple ball or tube beads on either side of the center bead.

CRAZY DOUGHS

Add sawdust and coffee grinds to dough? Sculpt with soap or sandwich bread? Concoct these doughs and you'll be convinced, crazy doughs are as practical as they are unusual.

★ SOAPY DOUGH ★

This dough has a very chunky texture. It's fine for projects that don't require a lot of details. An added benefit — the soapy sculptures you make can also help keep you clean!

WHAT YOU NEED

2 cups (500 ml) soap flakes

1/2 cup (125 ml) hot water

Eggbeater

WHAT YOU DO

1 Pour soap flakes and water into a bowl. Add a few drops of food coloring if you wish. Beat until evenly mixed.

2 Gather the mixture in your hands. Press it into a firm glob. Place the glob on a pie plate.

3 Shape in any way you like.

4 Let your project dry for several days. Enjoy it as sculpture or use it as soap.

★ SOAP-ON-A-ROPE ★

Soap-on-a-rope makes a great gift. Or, wear it yourself as you sing in the shower.

WHAT YOU NEED

Soapy dough, page 61

About 1 yard (90 cm) of yarn or cord

WHAT YOU DO

1 Cut a thick piece of yarn long enough to fit very loosely around your neck. Tie the ends together with a large knot.

2 Press a soap-size glob of Soapy Dough on the yarn just above the knot. Squeeze the glob so it hangs securely from the yarn. Form into a special shape such as a heart, a duck, a half moon, or blazing sun.

3 Let the soap dry for several days. Now tie another knot just where the yarn comes back out of the soap.

SOAPBERRIES

It's amazing what people use to get themselves clean! In some tropical parts of the world, native people use "soapberries" when they want to wash their hands. These berries lather right up when they're mixed with water.

ARTIST'S CHOICE!

Here are other ways to use Soapy Dough:

★ **Soap snow.** Soapy dough is perfect for making winter projects such as snowpeople or decorated snowballs. Put "snow" on the edges of pinecones for a festive decoration.

★ **Cuddly creatures.** Soapy dough is great for making cuddled-up creatures. A sleeping lamb will hold together much better than a standing lamb with spindly legs. Try making napping white animals such as kittens, rabbits, or swans. For a special gift, place a few soap animals in a basket atop a fluffy, new washcloth.

★ **Added touches.** To decorate your sculptures, stick buttons, beans, pipe cleaners, or other small colorful objects into them.

★ BREAD CRUMB DOUGH ★

This dough has a chunky, rustic look. It works nicely for small works of art such as beads, as well as larger pieces such as puppets. The dough dries with a smooth finish. When dry, paint pieces with a mixture of one spoonful of white glue mixed with one spoonful of water. Apply two or three coats. Let each coat dry before applying the next.

WHAT YOU NEED

3 slices of white bread

1–3 teaspoons (5–15 ml) white glue

1/2 teaspoon (2 ml) liquid detergent or 1 teaspoon (5 ml) glycerin

WHAT YOU DO

1 Remove bread crusts. (Give them to the birds.) Crumble bread into tiny crumbs by tearing it apart in your hands. Work over a mixing bowl.

2 Add liquid detergent and one tablespoon (15 ml) of glue. Mix well with your hands. Add more glue if it is needed to hold the dough together. (Different breads hold together differently.)

3 Gather the mixture together and knead. The more you knead, the less sticky the dough will become.

4 Wrap unused dough tightly in plastic to store, because it hardens quickly.

5 Let finished art air dry on waxed paper. Turn from time to time so they don't stick to the paper.

★ ALIEN GLOB PUPPETS ★

The thick, sticky quality of bread crumb dough makes it the perfect consistency for grabbing onto string. Embedding string in the dough allows you to make outrageous alien creatures with weird dangling parts. Use your puppets to entertain an audience of family and friends.

WHAT YOU NEED

Bread Crumb Dough, page 63

Tools of the Trade (see page 48)

String

Thin wooden sticks, dowels, or chopsticks

WHAT YOU DO

1 Think about the alien you'd like to make with wiggling, jointed parts to its body. Aliens can have any parts jointed: tongues, tails, or "zlobs."

2 Use one glob for the main body, another for the head, and more globs for strange appendages. Lay out the pieces the way you'd like them to go together.

3 Cut pieces of string long enough to go through each appendage and into the main body. Press them into the puppet parts. Push a long piece of hanging string in through the head. (Cut all string extra long. You can always trim it down after the dough dries.)

4 Make sure the string is fully covered with dough. Reshape the globs to make the body parts look just right. Use Tools of the Trade to add strange textures.

5 Let your alien dry completely. Knot the ends of the strings and trim. Color and finish as you like. Now attach the hanging string to a chopstick. Move the chopstick to operate your puppet. Make several aliens and let the space-age puppet show begin!

ARTIST'S CHOICE!

Don't stop at aliens. How about making an octopus with eight dangling legs? A horse could have its head, legs, and tail jointed. You can even joint a person for a traditional marionette.

- - - - - - - - - -

Insert a thin dowel through the bottom of the puppet. The jointed parts will wiggle when you shake the stick.

★ WOODY DOUGH ★

Use woody dough when you want the natural look of wood, clay, or stone. This dough is coarse, so it is best suited for chunky creations — pots, bowls (see page 116), and other simple pieces. Roll it flat for cookie cutter shapes. Let your art dry for two to three days. You can then smooth it with sandpaper and glaze it with a clear acrylic sealer to bring out the nice wooden finish.

WHAT YOU NEED

1 cup (250 ml) sawdust

1/2 cup (125 ml) flour

1/4 cup (50 ml) water

1 tablespoon (15 ml) liquid starch or white glue (optional)

Sieve or piece of screening

WHAT YOU DO

1 Sift the sawdust through the sieve. You only want sawdust in your dough — not splinters or chunks of wood.

2 Mix all ingredients together. Depending on the type of sawdust used, you might need to add more water or flour.

3 Gather the mixture in your hands. Press it into a firm glob.

4 Knead the glob until it feels like a workable dough.

PINOCCHIO

Why do people love the story of Pinocchio? It's probably because we like to dream that a piece of wood could really come to life. The magical story was written by the Italian author Carlo Collodi over 100 years ago.

But people have enjoyed puppets for an even longer time. Clay marionettes were found among the ancient ruins of Rome. Later, troupes of puppeteers traveled all over Italy using marionettes to tell stories of knights in shining armor. Sometimes marionettes were five feet tall (150 cm) and weighed over eighty pounds (35.5 kg). They had to be held up with iron rods and operated by strong puppeteers.

Do you hear any voices in that lump of Bread Crumb Dough? If so, mold it into a puppet!

WHAT IN THE WORLD?

What can be done with the millions of tons of sawdust produced from lumber mills each year? Lots of interesting stuff. Mounds of decaying sawdust are used to grow mushrooms. In Japan, people sweat away their health problems by being buried up to their necks in a mixture of sawdust and heat-producing chemicals. Plus, sawdust is added to cow feed to make it bulkier, bowling ball cores to make them lighter, and sprinkled on skating rinks to make the ice stronger. It's even been mixed with chemicals, cooked, and squeezed to make oil. Unfortunately, it takes three tons of sawdust to make one barrel of oil!

Then & Now

Huitzilopochtli, Aztec God of the Sun: Perhaps you've seen pictures of the huge, circular, Aztec calendar stone now displayed at the Museum of Anthropology in Mexico City. The bold face of the sun god, Huitzilopochtli, is carved in the center. The names of the twenty days of the Aztec month are also carved in the stone, along with Aztec ideas about the universe.

The sun was important to the ancient Aztecs of Mexico. They believed that the world had been created five times. The first four worlds and their suns had been destroyed. Aztecs held a "new fire" ceremony every 52 years to assure that their fifth world and its sun would be protected.

★ METEPEC SUN ★

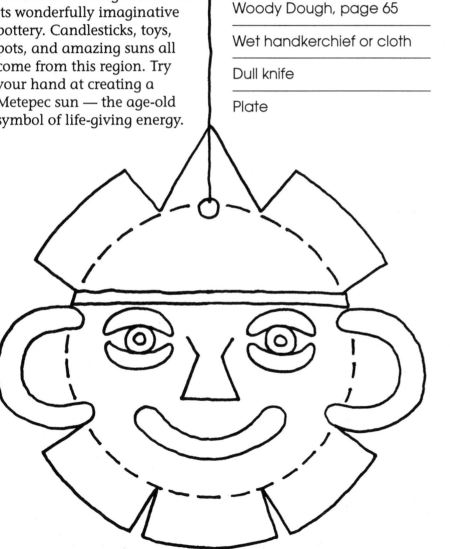

Metepec is a state in Mexico long famous for its wonderfully imaginative pottery. Candlesticks, toys, pots, and amazing suns all come from this region. Try your hand at creating a Metepec sun — the age-old symbol of life-giving energy.

WHAT YOU NEED

Woody Dough, page 65

Wet handkerchief or cloth

Dull knife

Plate

WHAT YOU DO

1 Although some Metepec suns are as large as 2 feet (60 cm) across, about 8 inches (20 cm) in diameter is a nice size to work with.

2 Place a wet cloth on the back of a plate. Roll out a slab of dough about ¾ inch (1 cm) thick and set it on top of the cloth. Or, press the dough onto the back of the cloth-covered plate. Cut the slab into a circle shape about the size of the plate.

3 Use both hands to pinch rays around the perimeter of the clay circle. Use your own technique or try these ways to make rays: add squiggles or triangles of dough or press a patterned texture into the edge. Be sure add-on rays are well joined and not too small and spindly or they may fall off when dry.

4 Now design the face. Use a dull knife to cut eye and mouth slits. Or, use pieces of clay snakes to build up the nose, eyebrows, cheeks, and other features. Or, do both.

5 Let your sun dry for several days. Traditional Metepec suns are often left unpainted.

ARTIST'S CHOICE!

If you'd like to paint your sun, try doing it the Metepec way. First paint the entire sun with white tempera. Let it dry. Then paint the facial features. Next add flower patterns to the cheeks and forehead.

★ COFFEE DOUGH ★

Coffee dough has a natural look when it dries. The brown color and coffee-grind speckles in this concoction will make your art work look as if it's made from stone.

WHAT YOU NEED

1 cup (250 ml) flour

1/2 cup (125 ml) salt

1 cup (250 ml) used coffee grinds

1/2 cup (125 ml) cold, left-over coffee

WHAT YOU DO

1 Combine all ingredients in a bowl. Stir until blended.

2 Gather the mixture together with your hands.

3 Knead on a floured surface until you have a smooth dough.

4 Store dough in a plastic bag or margarine tub.

WHERE IN THE WORLD?

There's an old legend told by Middle Easterners about a goatherder named Kaldi and the discovery of coffee. One day while tending to his flock, Kaldi noticed his goats were acting silly. When he ate some of the berries the goats were enjoying, Kaldi discovered why the goats were so excited — the berries were delicious and made him feel energized! Kaldi then told the world about his marvelous discovery, and that is how some believe coffee came to be.

YOU BE THE PALEONTOLOGIST

Examine the fossilized animal tracks before you. The first group of tracks are large, set deep in the rock, and far apart from each other. The other group of fossil tracks are small, close together, and not very deep in the rock. What can you discover about these animals?

You might put the clues together like this: The first animal must have been large and heavy to leave such deep tracks. Its legs must have been far apart on its body to make such a long stride; it must have been huge. The second animal was lighter, so its feet did not sink as deeply into the mud.

Lasting impressions: "Fossil" means dug up. And that's exactly what paleontologists do to find fossils. Fossils, which can be millions of years old, are formed in different ways. The fossils you might make on page 70 are similar to *mold fossils*. A piece of plant or animal gets buried; it leaves its impression in the mud. Over thousands of years the mud turns to rock. As the earth moves, ancient fossils come closer to the surface. Then they are found by paleontologists and people like you.

★ MAKE AN IMPRESSION ★

Coffee or tea leaf doughs are great for making fossils. Their speckled texture gives your "fossils" an authentic look.

WHAT YOU NEED

Coffee Dough, page 68

Can or dull knife

WHAT YOU DO

1 Roll dough to about 1/2 inch (1 cm) thick. Use a can to cut out a circular shape, or cut the slab into any shape you want.

2 Now press a special object or objects into the dough. Remove the object and you'll be left with its impression.

3 If you wish to hang the impression, be sure to make a hole with a nail or straw near the top before the slab dries.

Use the parts of your hand to recreate the footprint of a real or imaginary animal (see Mystery Tracks, page 44). Instead of making a print with paint, press your nails, fingertips, or the edge of your hand into the dough to leave an impression.

The following make interesting impressions:

★ Leaves

★ Twigs

★ Your hand

★ Your baby-sister's foot

★ Nuts and bolts

★ Shells

★ Kitchen gadgets

★ Pet's paw print

★ TEA LEAF DOUGH ★

This is a nice dough to use when you want to create small art works and beads that have a natural stone appearance.

WHAT YOU NEED

4 tablespoons (50 ml) flour

1 tablespoon (15 ml) salt

1 tablespoon (15 ml) water

About 2 tablespoons (25 ml) used tea leaves or petal crumble (see Art Smart!)

WHAT YOU DO

1 Mix flour, salt, and water in a bowl.

2 Add as many tea leaves as the dough will hold without falling apart.

3 Gather the mixture in your hands. Press it into a firm ball.

4 Put the ball on a clean surface and knead until you have a smooth dough.

Art Smart

Petal Crumble: Collect dried flower petals. (Rose petals work well; ask a florist to save some roses that have gone by for you to use.) Crumble petals into a bowl by tearing them apart and rubbing them between your hands. Add this petal crumble to the dough instead of tea leaves. Use the dough to make small bud-shaped beads (see Jazzy Jewelry, page 59). String them to make a beautiful flower petal dough necklace.

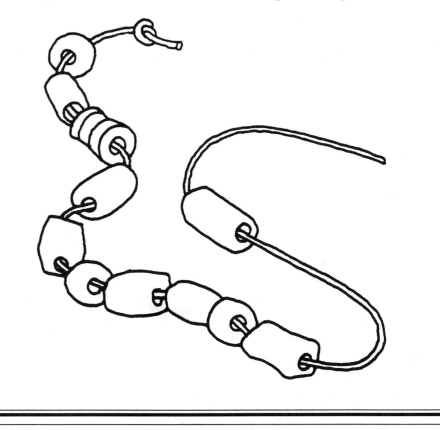

★ ZUNI ANIMAL FETISH ★

Since ancient times Zuni artists of North America have carved animal fetishes (very small animal sculptures) from stone. They believed the fetish held the spirit of the animal it represented. That spirit could be very valuable to the one who possessed the fetish. It could offer powerful help in hunting, healing, and protection.

WHAT YOU NEED

Tea Leaf Dough, page 71

Flour Dough, page 46–47

Twine

Toothpick

WHAT YOU DO

1 Make a ball of tea leaf dough small enough to fit in your hand. Think about your favorite wild animal as you mold its image from the dough. What special powers does your animal possess? Can it change the course of a river like a beaver? Can it glide more than 100 feet like a flying squirrel? Can it frighten its enemy with a sudden display of color like the fire-bellied toad?

2 Use flour dough to make an arrow-shaped piece — small enough to fit onto the animal's back. Use a toothpick to press a channel into the arrow where it will hold the twine.

3 Place the arrow on the animal's back and let both pieces dry together.

4 When dry, tie twine around the arrow and the animal to hold the arrow in place.

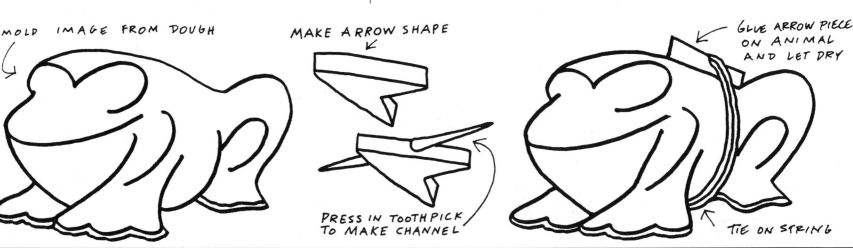

MOLD IMAGE FROM DOUGH

MAKE ARROW SHAPE

PRESS IN TOOTHPICK TO MAKE CHANNEL

GLUE ARROW PIECE ON ANIMAL AND LET DRY

TIE ON STRING

STICKY STUFF

Imagine a world without adhesives — all those substances that stick things together. We'd come unglued! Adhesives are incredibly useful. They can hold violins together, bind books, and even keep the grains on sandpaper.

LICK-IT-LATER STICKER GUMS

Create Lick-It-Later Sticker Gums when you want to make something easy to stick in the future. Spread the gum thinly on the back of a small picture. Let it dry. Moisten the back when you are ready to stick the picture onto cardboard or paper. Sticker gums are perfect for making your own stickers, seals, labels, stamps, and envelopes.

Lick-It-Later Gum I is made from a packet of unflavored gelatin. Lick-It-Later Gum II is made from instant dessert gelatin. They both gel nicely onto paper. Use whichever type of gelatin you have handy.

★ LICK-IT-LATER GUM I ★

WHAT YOU NEED

1 packet (1/4 oz or 6.25 g) unflavored gelatin

1/4 cup (50 ml) boiling water

1 tablespoon (15 ml) sugar

1/4 teaspoon (1 ml) food flavoring (optional)

WHAT YOU DO

1 Pour gelatin into a heat-proof container. Ask a grown-up to add the boiling water. Stir with a fork until gelatin is dissolved.

2 Add sugar and stir until dissolved.

3 Add flavoring such as vanilla, maple, or lemon. Or, add a few drops of peppermint oil. Stir.

★ LICK-IT-LATER GUM II ★

WHAT YOU NEED

1 tablespoon (15 ml) flavored gelatin mix

2 tablespoons (25 ml) boiling water

WHAT YOU DO

1 Pour gelatin into a heat-proof container.

2 Ask a grown-up to add the boiling water. Stir with a fork until gelatin is dissolved.

Art Smart

When the gum in your container sets into a hard gelatin, simply set the container in a pan of hot water to turn back to a liquid.

ARTIST'S CHOICE!

Brush sticker gum onto the back of a small picture. Let dry. Later you can stick your picture on paper by just licking or wetting the back.

- - - - - - - - - -

These mixtures also work as "Stick-It-Now" gums. Brush them on the back of any paper you want to stick down.

★ CUSTOM-DESIGNED STICKERS ★

WHAT YOU NEED

Small drawings or magazine pictures

Pair of scissors

Lick-It-Later Gum I or II

Small paintbrush

Design a set of stickers just for you or as a gift for a special person. Use them to personalize and add pizzazz to any sheet of paper or envelope.

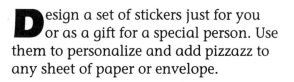

WHAT YOU DO

1 Collect or draw small, interesting pictures. Cut them out. You can also cut out basic shapes, such as stars, circles, or triangles from Special Papers (see page 132) or from magazines.

2 Spread the backs with Lick-It-Later Gum I or II. Let the gum dry.

3 Moisten the back when you wish to stick your sticker.

PRESSING MATTERS

Hundreds of years ago, people didn't have the self-sealing envelopes we use today. Instead, hot wax was pressed between paper to seal it. When the hot wax cooled, it glued the paper together.

Next time you mail a letter to someone, try using wax to seal the envelope. Have a grown-up light a candle and gently drip some of the wax onto the envelope's seal. Then close it quickly before the wax dries. Or, do what people did before self-sealing envelopes existed — drip some wax on it, then quickly imprint a decorative button or coin in the wax. You'll leave your very own personalized imprint!

PAPER PASTES

Mix a little flour with a little water, and you've concocted an amazingly sticky adhesive. *Gluten*, the substance in flour that holds bread together, also gives flour paste its sticking power. The concoctions in this section are pastes that work well for gluing paper. Mix them up, and then try them out on some Sticky Stuff projects.

★ SUGAR PASTE ★

WHAT YOU NEED

1/4 cup (50 ml) sugar

1/4 cup (50 ml) flour

1 cup (250 ml) water

WHAT YOU DO

1 Mix sugar, flour, and water in a pot.

2 Ask a grown-up to help you with the cooking. Keep stirring as you heat the mixture.

3 Simmer until the mixture looks like pudding.

4 Store in a covered container in the refrigerator.

★ CORNSTARCH PASTE ★

WHAT YOU NEED

2 tablespoons (25 ml) sugar

½ cup (125 ml) cornstarch

1 cup (250 ml) water

WHAT YOU DO

1 Mix cornstarch and sugar with a little bit of the water in a pot. Stir until it forms a paste.

2 Gradually add the rest of the water and stir.

3 Ask a grown-up to help you cook the mixture until it looks like pudding.

4 Store in a covered container in the refrigerator.

CHICKEN GLUE?

Have you ever noticed the puddle of jelly around a cold chicken from last night's dinner? That's a form of glue. Some glues are made from bones, hides, and sinews. These natural materials are heated, processed, and dried to make a glue powder. The craftsperson adds water to the powder and starts sticking!

STICKY ART

A cupful of paste, a few sheets of paper, and a pair of scissors — that's all you need for these fun cut-and-paste creations. Spread just a little paste evenly on the back of the paper so that it dries smooth and wrinkle-free.

In French, the word collage means to "paste up" different materials, creating something artistic in the process. You can use just about anything to make a collage: magazine pages, old greeting cards, photos, advertisements. A collage makes a statement about how you feel. Why not make a layered picture about the environment, friendship, peace, or anything that's important to you.

WHAT YOU NEED

Poster board or heavy paper for the backing, magazines

Colored paper scraps

Scissors

Paper paste, page 77–78

★ COLLAGE ★

1 Look through magazines for pictures and messages about your subject. Tear or cut them out. You can also add pieces of solid-colored paper or even three-dimensional items like buttons with slogans or a dried flower or a shell.

2 Arrange items in an interesting way on the poster board. If you can't find the words you want, cut out letters from different words to make your own words and sentences. Sometimes an advertising slogan about one thing can be used for something else. For example, a slogan for dishwashing liquid, "Let's Clean Up!" can become a message in an environmental collage. Let your imagination run wild. A flower can grow out of a person's body. Words can come out of a baby's mouth. Horses can gallop through the sky. You decide.

3 Once you're pleased with the way your collage looks, paste it down.

Art SMART

Collages make wonderful gifts or greeting cards when they contain references to the interests and events of the recipient's life. Make a jam-packed collage for someone very special in your life. That person is sure to treasure it forever.

BRAQUE'S WAY

The French artist Georges Braque created outrageous collages during the early 1900s that have become very famous. He cut and pasted together materials that most people would have simply tossed in the wastebasket. His famous *Le Courrier* is a collage made from such materials as newspaper and a tobacco wrapper!

You can make unusual collages that are great examples of recycled art, making use of all sorts of odds and ends. So, start saving those foil-lined gum wrappers, a special shell, a pressed flower — even the label from a can of soup. It all makes great art when combined with your own ingenuity!

★ TORN PAPER MOSAICS ★

Mosaics are usually made from clay tiles, but you can make your own tiles from cut or torn paper.

WHAT YOU NEED

Poster board or heavy paper for a backing

Magazines or colored paper scraps

Pencil

Scissors

Paper paste, (see page 77–78)

WHAT YOU DO

1 Lightly sketch a picture by outlining simple shapes, such as a sailboat on water with the sun overhead. Draw areas where you want each color to be.

2 Tear or cut scraps of colored paper into "tiles," or small squares. Make separate piles for each color.

3 Spread paste onto the back of a tile. Stick it onto the poster board. Do not overlap the tiles. Let a thin line of white poster board show around each tile. Repeat until your mosaic is covered with paper tiles.

ARTIST'S CHOICE!

Try different kinds of paper for your mosaics. You can make something very beautiful using torn tissue paper, or try some shiny foil gift wrap for a shimmering night scene. Be adventurous and combine different kinds of paper for a fantastic mosaic!

ART SMART

Look through old magazines for photos of the colors you want to use in your mosaic. For example, if you are hunting for blue, you might use the sky from one picture, clothing from another, or a lake from another. Then, make separate piles for each shade of blue. Using different shades of a color — like several blues to make your own sky or ocean — is a real challenge that results in wonderful torn paper mosaics.

★ ART QUAKE ★

WHAT YOU NEED

Two contrasting colors of paper (such as black and white or yellow and red)

Scissors

Paper paste, (see page 77–78)

WHAT YOU DO

1 Cut one sheet into a large, interesting shape. Then cut that shape into unusual pieces.

2 Put the pieces back together like a puzzle on the uncut sheet. Leave spaces between each small piece. Let the bold color of the uncut sheet show through.

3 Paste down the pieces when you are happy with the way they are spaced. How's that for art that really moves you!

Create an "art quake" by cutting apart a shape. Then paste it back together leaving spaces in between each piece. Notice how the spaces give energy and movement to your piece of art.

ARTIST'S CHOICE!

Try "art quaking" a magazine photo. Cut it into strips. Paste the strips down, in order, on construction paper. Don't let the strips line up exactly with each other. Let the construction paper show between each strip. The new photo will look as if it's been through an art quake!

MIRROR ★ MIRROR

Learn about *negative space* (the area that surrounds shapes you draw or cut out) as you make a bold, mirrored design.

WHAT YOU NEED

Two contrasting colors of paper (such as red and green or black and orange)

Scissors

Paper paste, (see page 77–78)

WHAT YOU DO

1 Cut one sheet in half. Fold the half-sheet down the middle. Hold the outside edge as you cut a shape from the fold. You can also cut shapes from the edges. Save all scraps.

2 Open the paper you cut from. Lay it out on one half of the uncut sheet of contrasting paper.

3 Open up the shape and scraps you cut out. Lay them out on the other half of the contrasting paper in the same arrangement as the paper you cut them from.

4 Paste the large piece and the scraps from which it was cut side by side on the contrasting paper.

You now have an interesting image that is bold and *symmetrical* (one side mirrors the other).

★ STANDING CREATURES ★

Make a zoo full of real or imaginary creatures.

WHAT YOU NEED

Several colors of paper

Scissors

Paper paste,
(see page 77–78)

WHAT YOU DO

1 Fold a sheet of paper in half.

2 Hold the fold as you cut legs and body parts from the outside edge. You can also cut into the fold — just don't cut all the way through.

3 Heads or tails can be cut from scraps. Join them by cutting a slit in the folded edge and inserting the piece. Or, paste them on.

4 Cut out feathers, whiskers, fins, eyes, stripes, blotches, and other details from scraps of colored paper. Paste these onto your creature.

5 Unfold part way to stand your creature up.

The display's the thing:
A good technique for displaying your art is to group related items together for both artistic and decorative impact. With Standing Creatures, you can create three to five different animals and group them as if they are grazing. That would be a good arrangement because the art technique of cutting and pasting the animals unifies the group.

Another way to display art is to take a theme — such as fish — and then display perhaps a clay fish, a papier-mache fish, a fish made from paper tile art, and perhaps a standing animal fish. In this technique, the subject, rather than the process, is the unifying feature.

MOLDING PASTES

Molding pastes are great when you want to shape paper and hold it together at the same time. This is what you do with papier-mache. Use these pastes for both strip and mash papier-mache projects (see pages 99–100). Try either paste out by making the Comical Sun Hat on page 86.

Molding pastes can also be used for basic paper-sticking. The instant variety lets you get started right away without grown-up help. The cooked kind is a bit smoother and nicer to work with. Both types work well.

★ INSTANT FLOUR MOLDING PASTE ★

WHAT YOU NEED

½ cup (125 ml) flour

½ cup (125 ml) water

WHAT YOU DO

1 Stir flour and water together in a bowl. The paste should look thick and creamy. Add more water or flour, if necessary.

2 Store in a container in the refrigerator.

★ COOKED FLOUR MOLDING PASTE ★

WHAT YOU NEED

1/2 cup (125 ml) flour

2 tablespoons (25 ml) sugar

2 cups (500 ml) water

WHAT YOU DO

1 Stir flour, sugar, and water together in the pot.

2 Ask a grown-up to help you heat and stir the mixture until it boils.

3 Cook and stir until thick.

4 Store in a container in the refrigerator.

Made to order: Imagine a special hat, made just for you. The milliner (hat-maker) steams a piece of wool felt. Then she or he shapes it on a wooden form the size of your head. The brim is then molded to suit you. Next the milliner adds the ribbons and silk flowers of your choice.

Fifty years ago my grandmother would have made that special hat just for you in her little shop in New York City. Today, you can make your own hat by molding paper instead of wool. Pretend you are a top fashion designer as you decorate your creation.

★ COMICAL SUN HAT ★

Make a colorful, lightweight hat that fits you perfectly!

WHAT YOU NEED

Two sheets of Sunday comic paper

Flour Molding Paste, pages 84–85

Scissors

String

WHAT YOU DO

1 Cut both sheets of paper into huge squares.

CUT OUT A LARGE SQUARE

2 Spread paste evenly over the entire surface of one square. Place the other sheet on top and press them together.

SPREAD GLUE ON 1 SQUARE ONLY

PLACE THIS SQUARE ON TOP OF GLUE-COVERED SQUARE

3 You now have a large, damp, paper square that looks nothing like a hat. Change that by putting the square on your head. Have a helper mold the hat to fit your head and have an overall shape that you want. Now have your helper tie a string around it to hold the shape. The limp brim will droop in your face. Keep this contraption on your head for about 10 minutes. If you feel ridiculous, have your helper join you by making a hat, too. Now sing silly songs together and tell "knock-knock" jokes while you wait.

4 Take the paper off your head being careful not to change its new shape. Leave it on a flat surface in a warm place so the brim can dry flat. Do not disturb until it's dry.

5 After the hat is dry and rigid, remove the string. Cut the edge of the paper brim to form any shape you like.

LET DRY

REMOVE STRING

CUT BRIM

6 Place hat on your head and enjoy a walk in the sun!

ARTIST'S CHOICE!

Make the hat from large pieces of gift-wrapping paper.

– – – – – – – – – –

Make the hat from regular newspaper. See papier-mache decorating, page 102, for ways to jazz up your creation.

– – – – – – – – – –

Comical hats make great party hats for summer parties. Have your guests make them as the first party activity. Let them dry in the sun. They should be ready to decorate and enjoy toward the end of the party.

★ MOLDED MENAGERIE ★

Make a menagerie of animals from a moldable "paste and paper sandwich." Arrange on a shelf or make your creatures into a mobile (see page 141).

WHAT YOU NEED

Flour Molding Paste, pages 84–85

Two sheets of the same size paper

Stapler

WHAT YOU DO

1 Spread paste all over a sheet of paper.

2 Lay another sheet of paper on top to make a "paste and paper sandwich." You now have a damp sheet of paper from which to form an animal.

3 Mold the paper as you like. It will dry rigid in the shape you created.

TRY MAKING THESE EASY ANIMAL SHAPES:

Bird. Accordion-fold the sandwich. Put a staple at one end to form the beak. Staple a couple of inches from the beak to form the head, and a couple of inches from the other end to form the tail. Spread out the center sections so they look like a head and body. Accordion-fold another sandwich to make wings. Staple the center. Fan out the sides. Attach them to the body with hanging string. Have a grown-up help you use a needle to poke a string through both the wings and body. Or, attach the wings with paste after the parts are dry.

Butterfly. Accordion-fold the sandwich. Wrap a pipe cleaner around the center to form the body. Fan out the two sides to make the wings.

Fish. Accordion-fold the sandwich. Put a staple at one end to form the mouth. Staple a couple of inches from the other end to form the tail. Spread out the center section to form the body. Fan out the tail.

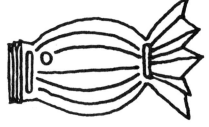

Snake. Spread paste all over a sheet of newspaper. Make a long tube by rolling the paper diagonally from a corner. Now coil the tube into a snake shape. Lift the head section and drape it over a cup to hold its shape as it dries.

ARTIST'S CHOICE!

Use any of these papers for your molded creatures:

★ Colored paper

★ Newspaper

★ Magazine pages

★ Special papers you've made throughout this book

Decorate with tempera or leave plain.

PAPER CAPERS

The concoctions in Paper Capers focus on fabulous fibers. Gather them from old newspaper, greeting cards, and even egg cartons. Recycle them into handsome, handmade paper. Mash them into papier-mache creatures. See for yourself what the fibers in crepe paper, napkins, and even toilet paper are like to mold!

What's paper made of? Tear a piece and see. Look closely at the torn edge. It looks sort of hairy, doesn't it? These hairs are *plant fibers* — the same as those that make a plant's roots, leaves, and stems strong. Next time you doodle on a notepad, think about how you are drawing on top of millions of plant fibers! That's how many it takes to make a sheet of paper.

What keeps those millions of tiny fibers from falling apart? Ah, that's the wonderful thing about *cellulose*, the special substance plant fibers are made of. Cellulose fibers stick to each other very easily. It's this sticking trait that causes them to mat together into a sheet of paper when water is added to them. Then, when you take the water away by drying, almost magically the bond becomes even stronger. Tug at the sides of a dry sheet of paper; it's amazingly strong, isn't it? It's almost impossible to pull those fibers apart!

HANDMADE PAPERS

You know you need fibers to make paper, but where can you get them? How about from the recycled fibers of used pieces of paper! Tear the paper apart and mix with water to get a new bond started. Catch those fibers on a screen to form a mat. Remove the water by letting the mat dry. Presto! That's all it takes to make a beautiful sheet of handmade paper!

REEDIN' AND WRITIN'

Four thousand years ago Egyptians got tired of carrying around messages carved in heavy stone. They looked no further than their own Nile River for a new idea. There, on the river's banks, towered 12-foot (4 m) reeds called *papyrus*. The triangular-shaped papyrus stems were cut into thin strips and laid side by side. Another layer was laid cross-wise on top of the first. The layers were pounded to release a gluelike plant sap that held the layers together.

The idea of a cheap, lightweight writing mat that rolled up easily soon became all the rage. Egyptians sold papyrus mats throughout the world. Even the word *paper* comes from the Egyptian word *papyrus*.

★ MAKE-YOUR-OWN PAPER ★

Making your own papers is lots of fun and one of the ultimate concoctions. However, please don't pour leftover pulp down the sink. It will clog the drain.

WHAT YOU NEED

Scrap paper

Water

2 wooden frames (the same size and small enough to fit in a washtub with plenty of room to spare)

Nylon screening

Wash basin

Tacks

Blender (for grown-up use only)

Old newspaper

2 small towels

WHAT YOU DO

1 To make sheets of paper, you need a *mold* and *deckle*. Use picture frames (without the glass) or canvas stretch bars. Cover one frame tightly with the nylon screening; then tack it down. You will use this frame as the *mold* to lift the pulp from the water. The other frame, the *deckle*, gives the paper an even edge.

DECKLE →

SCREEN

STAPLE OR TACK SCREEN TO MOLD

2 Tear scrap paper into small pieces. Soak the paper in a bowl of water until thoroughly wet. Fill the blender half full with the mixture, then beat those fibers to a pulp! Blend until no chunks remain.

3 Fill the basin about 1/4 full of water. Pour the pulp into the basin until it is about 3/4 full.

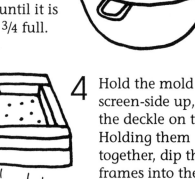

4 Hold the mold screen-side up, with the deckle on top. Holding them together, dip the frames into the basin and scoop up some pulp. Gently move the mold and deckle back and forth until the pulp is an even layer on the screen.

5 Set on newspaper and let the water drain away. Remove the deckle, and lay a towel on top of the handmade paper. Carefully turn the towel, paper, and mold over onto the table.

TOWEL

PAPER

MOLD

6 Use a sponge to remove excess water from the back of the screen. Lift mold, and leave the paper on the towel. Blot with another towel.

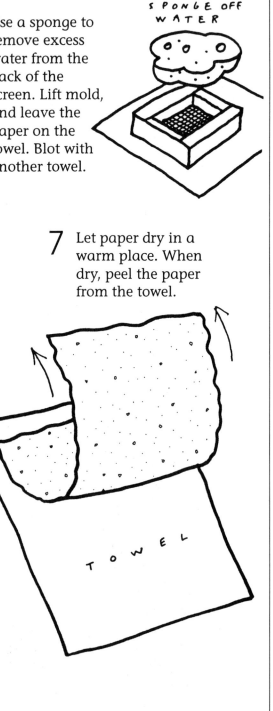

SPONGE OFF WATER

7 Let paper dry in a warm place. When dry, peel the paper from the towel.

TOWEL

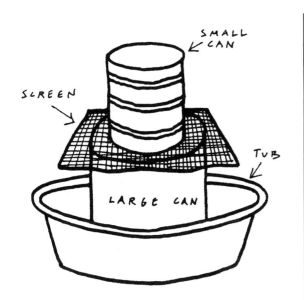

SMALL CAN

SCREEN

LARGE CAN

TUB

No Frames? Try Tin Cans.

1 Cut both ends from two different-sized tin cans, taking care not to cut yourself. Set cans in a tub or bowl, with the smaller can on top of the larger one. Place a piece of screening in between as shown.

2 Pour enough pulp mixture into the top can so that a small round sheet sits on the screen.

3 Remove the top can. Set the screen on a dry washcloth. Place another washcloth on top. Flip it over on the table. Remove the top cloth.

4 Follow steps 6 and 7 on page 92 for removing excess water and drying. You now have a unique circle of handmade paper! Different-sized cans will make different-sized circles of paper.

★ No blender? You can get good results beating the pulp concoction with a whisk or eggbeater.

★ Each time you dip into the pulp concoction, the paper sheets will get thinner. This is because you are using up more and more of the pulp. Add pulp to the concoction from time to time.

★ Try these ways to speed up the drying process: Keep your sheet sandwiched between two towels after step 6, page 92. Place some heavy books on the towel, or roll a rolling pin over the towel to squeeze out more water. Or, have a grown-up iron your paper on a medium setting while it's sandwiched between two towels. Gently place it on a fresh towel to finish drying.

Benjamin Franklin bought rags?:
If you lived in America 200 years ago, Benjamin Franklin might have paid you three cents a pound for your old rags. Mr. Franklin was a rag buyer for paper mills. For more than 500 years, most paper in Europe and North America came from worn-out clothes made of cotton and linen. Linen comes from flax plants and cotton comes from cotton plants. So rags are full of plant fibers — just right for making paper!

Now more and more paper is made from recycled paper — newspaper, computer paper, magazines, catalogs. Even 200 years ago, people knew that recycling made a lot of good sense!

DESIGNER SHEETS

The art of paper-making is to create sheets of paper like no other. The fun comes from making those sheets from creative pulp concoctions. Papers of the master paper-makers are unique pieces of art. You can be a master paper-maker, too. Hunt for unusual fibers to make your sheets into one-of-a-kind masterpieces.

The sort of pulp you concoct determines the type of sheet you'll get. Experiment with many kinds of scrap paper. Use each kind separately or mix several kinds together. (Black print from newspaper causes sheets to be dull gray. Also, you can use glossy papers, but the results aren't quite as nice.)

FIBER SOURCES

Greeting cards: These contain fine paper-making fibers. Save them!

Product packaging: Cereal boxes and more

Junk mail: You've heard that "one person's junk is another person's treasure." Here's proof of that! Save those catalogs and brochures.

Gift wrapping

Comics

Shopping bags

Old playing cards

Old road maps

Tissues and napkins

Magazines

Computer printouts

SPECIAL EFFECTS

You can make truly special, distinctive papers by using one of these special effects or experimenting on your own. If you enjoy concocting, experimenting, and making art, paper-making is one of the most expressive forms you'll come across.

★ **Colored paper:** Save solid-colored parts of greeting cards and envelopes or construction paper scraps. Use one color for paper-making. Or, color the water with food coloring. (This works well when using white or light-colored papers.)

★ **White paper:** Cut away print from envelopes and greeting cards. Cut margins from office paper.

★ **Splotches of color:** Stop the blender before it can completely grind up all of the paper so that some of the pieces are larger. These will appear as splotches of color on your sheet. Leave bits of words here and there on your sheets.

★ **Crepe paper:** If you want to make some spectacular paper, add torn bits of crepe paper or tissue gift wrap to your pulp concoction. Don't blend. Make special occasion paper — like red, white, and blue for Fourth of July!

★ **Special specks:** Sprinkle any of these items onto the deckle or mix into pulp mixture after blended: colored threads, bits of ribbon, lint from the dryer, bits of clean foil, thin leaves, tea leaves, flower petals, glitter, postage stamps.

★ **Embossing:** Press a leaf or coin into the sheet before it is ironed or weighted (see Art Smart on page 93 for ways to speed up the drying process). You can make a unique embossing symbol by cutting a shape from lightweight cardboard or coiling a piece of wire.

★ **Scented paper:** If you would like to develop a trademark scent, add a few drops of your favorite scent to the pulp.

Small bundles of handmade paper tied together with ribbon or twine make lovely gifts.

MULBERRY BARK AND FISHING NETS

T'sai Lun of ancient China was a very imaginative inventor. He gathered old rags, bits of rope, and fishing nets, then added mulberry bark and boiled it all in water. He mashed his brew to tear the fibers apart and make a pulp. Then he used a strainer to lift the pulp from the water. The matted fibers were dried in the sun to make the first sheet of true paper. Who would have ever thought that the way T'sai Lun made his crazy concoction 2000 years ago would be much the same way paper is made in paper mills today!

PAPER BOWLS

Make lovely, delicate paper bowls from a colorful pulp concoction. These bowls are perfect for holding paper clips, stamps, small treasures, or special stones.

WHAT YOU NEED

Paper pulp (see Make-Your-Own Paper, page 92)

Nonstick cooking spray

Clear acrylic sealer (optional)

Sieve

Dull knife

Small bowl

Make two or three batches of pulp in different colors. For an interesting splotchy effect, press patches of different-colored pulp together on the same bowl.

WHAT YOU DO

1 Use a sieve to strain the water from a blender full of paper pulp. Press the pulp against the sieve to remove more water.

2 Spray the inside of the bowl with nonstick cooking spray.

3 Press a layer of pulp against the inside of the bowl. Cover the inside completely. Do not let the original bowl show through.

4 Let the pulp dry in a warm, dry place. Use a dull knife to loosen the paper bowl from the original bowl.

5 Paint with clear acrylic sealer to protect and strengthen.

Unlikely umbrellas: Most of the umbrellas you see today are made from cloth or plastic, but the earliest umbrellas were actually made from paper. Oil was brushed on to make them waterproof.

PAPIER-MACHE

In French, *papier-mache* means "chewed paper" — and, in a sense, that's just the way papier-mache is made. Papier-mache is really another form of recycling old paper. Unlike handmade papers, with papier-mache the artist isn't forming new paper from old, but instead is reusing old paper to make something entirely new.

Papier-mache is surprisingly strong and long-lasting. In fact, papier-mache furniture was strong enough for small children to use. Objects made 200 years ago are still useful today.

Two choices: There are two easy ways to use papier-mache. You can make a concoction of pulpy *mash* with paper and paste, and then shape it like a dough, any way you like. Or, you can build with *strips* of paper and paste around an object, or *form*. Either way, your dried art will be a lightweight sculpture, ready to decorate and enjoy.

★ PAPIER-MACHE PASTE ★

Paste is what holds your torn or "chewed" paper together. The instant variety lets you get started without grown-up help. The cooked paste is a bit smoother and nicer to work with. Either of these, or wallpaper paste, will do the job just great.

Instant Flour Paste (see page 84)

Cooked Flour Paste (see page 85)

Wallpaper paste (follow directions on package)

GIVE IT SHAPE!

The *form* is the basic shape that you will build on to create your papier-mache sculpture from strips. A form is like a skeleton because it gives the body structure. Make any kind of form with any kind of material, just so long as it holds together until the papier-mache is dry. Tape different items together. No one will see the tape or any part of the form when it's covered with papier-mache. Try combining some of these materials to make a form:

★ Crumpled paper or foil

★ Cardboard boxes or toilet-paper rolls in many sizes: large and small cereal boxes, school milk cartons, cracker boxes, toothpaste cartons

★ Tightly rolled tubes of newspaper

★ Coat hanger wire bent into shapes

★ Pieces of wood

★ Inflated balloons in different sizes

★ Chicken wire for huge pieces. You'll need grown-up help here.

Combine these items with masking tape into a free-form or realistic sculpture. Then cover with papier-mache. People, creatures, bananas, or rockets — they all can be made of papier-mache (see Dough Sculpture, page 49 for more ideas).

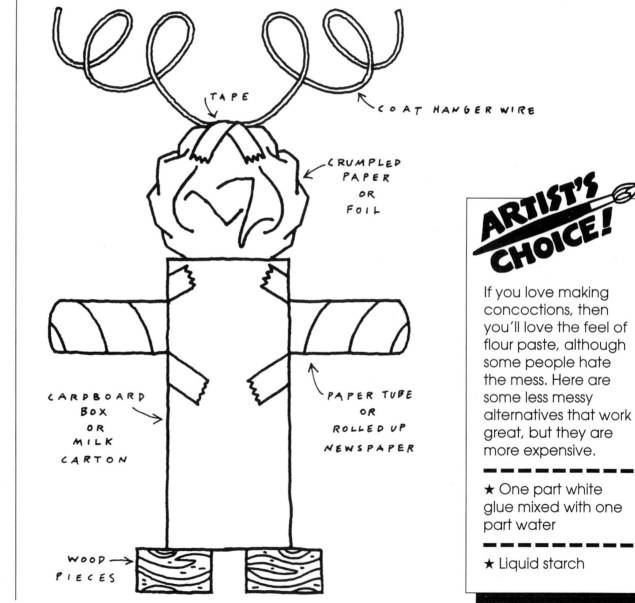

TAPE

COAT HANGER WIRE

CRUMPLED PAPER OR FOIL

CARDBOARD BOX OR MILK CARTON

PAPER TUBE OR ROLLED UP NEWSPAPER

WOOD PIECES

ARTIST'S CHOICE!

If you love making concoctions, then you'll love the feel of flour paste, although some people hate the mess. Here are some less messy alternatives that work great, but they are more expensive.

- - - - - - - -

★ One part white glue mixed with one part water

- - - - - - - -

★ Liquid starch

★ STRIPS ★

Strips are great for "cover-up" jobs. Make a form, then use strips to cover it up and hold the sculpture together. While mash dries bumpy and rough, dried strips form a smooth surface. Choose the look that's best for your sculpture.

WHAT YOU NEED

Newspapers

Any of the flour, glue, or starch pastes

WHAT YOU DO

1 Tear newspaper into strips about 1 inch (2.5 cm) wide by about 4 inches (10 cm) long.

2 Put paste in a flat bowl. Slide the strip through the paste.

3 Use one hand to hold the strip. Use the first two fingers of your other hand to squeeze out the excess paste.

4 Place the strip over the form. Repeat with enough strips to complete the layer, overlapping the strips as you go.

5 It's best to let each layer dry overnight before adding the next.

WASPS DO IT!

Imagine building a home of papier-mache? Well, wasps actually do! They are the true inventors of "chewed-paper" construction. The female's powerful jaws scrape wood from fences, barns — just about anywhere she can find it. She adds her saliva as a sort of paste, and presto! — a paper concoction that makes a great home.

The female wasp builds a beautiful nest that hangs from a plant stem or roof. The nest is a comb of hexagons. Each hexagon-shaped (six-sided) cell makes a snug papier-mache room for one of her eggs.

★ THE MASH ★

Here is a popular concoction for a basic mash. For two other mash concoctions that create great special effects, see page 51.

WHAT YOU NEED

Newspapers

Water

Any flour paste recipe

WHAT YOU DO

1 Tear newspaper into small pieces about 1 inch (2.5 cm) square. Soak overnight in twice as much water as newspaper.

2 Drain and squeeze out excess water.

3 Put pulp back in bowl. Add enough paste to hold the pulp together.

4 Knead the mash until it is workable. Add flour if it feels too wet. Start molding!

5 Let the finished creation dry outdoors or in a well-ventilated area. Then decorate.

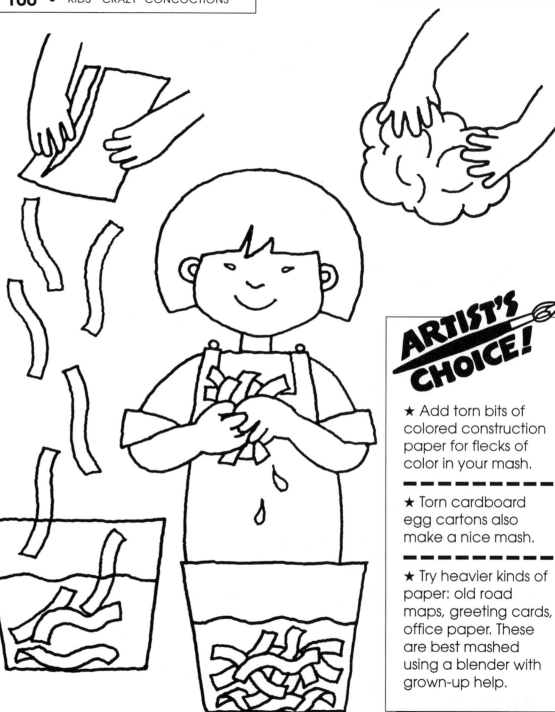

ARTIST'S CHOICE!

★ Add torn bits of colored construction paper for flecks of color in your mash.

- - - - - - - -

★ Torn cardboard egg cartons also make a nice mash.

- - - - - - - -

★ Try heavier kinds of paper: old road maps, greeting cards, office paper. These are best mashed using a blender with grown-up help.

SEGAL'S WAY

Modern artists quickly discovered that creating sculpture from papier-mache and other materials was a great way to make lifelike, three-dimensional works of art. George Segal, an artist who worked in the 1960s, created sculptures using plaster, Plexiglas™, and other materials. Sometimes he used live models to make his plaster casts. Segal's work most often showed ordinary people doing everyday tasks. His piece titled "Cinema," is a life-size sculpture of a man putting letters on a movie theater marquee.

PAPER DOUGH

Treat mash like a paper dough. It can be pressed onto or into molds or freely molded into your own shapes.

★ To prevent sticking, coat the form you wish to copy, such as a bowl, with petroleum jelly. Press the mash onto the form. Let dry. Then, gently pry the dried mash off with a blunt knife.

★ Coat the mold you wish to fill, such as a candy or gelatin mold, with petroleum jelly. Press the mash into the mold. Again, pry out with a blunt knife when dry.

★ Simply mold mash, like dough, into funny folks and creatures.

★ PAPIER-MACHE PIZZAZZ ★

Whether you made a mash or strip sculpture, be sure it is perfectly dry before you decorate it. Let your imagination run wild when it comes to decoration. You can paint your creation any way you like. Also consider pasting stuff on for texture.

★ **Paint:** Paint with thick tempera (see page 19). Bright colors keep the newsprint from showing through. Doughy paints (see page 29) are nice for adding details. If you have a problem with the newsprint showing through, paste on a layer of white paper towels or white tissue paper before painting.

★ **Paper patchwork:** A layer of colored tissue paper makes a bold, patchwork finish. Tear tissue paper into small pieces. Paint liquid starch where you want to stick pieces. Keep adding layers until you cannot see through to the newspaper. Brightly colored magazine photographs give a patchwork collage look. Tear the magazine photos into small bits. Paste on with a concoction of one part white glue and one part water. Be sure the pieces overlap.

★ **Texture:** Use white glue to paste on textures for animal skin or free-form pieces: rice, lentils or other dried foods, buttons, paper clips, seeds, or any small objects can be pasted on in interesting patterns. Paste them on after you paint and they will add to the color of your sculpture, too. Or, paste items on first and then cover everything with paint. This gives a unique, textured look to your sculpture.

★ **Coiled string or lace:** Use white glue to paste on string, coiled into interesting shapes. Then paint the entire piece, including the string, in one color. The string will make a raised design. You can do the same thing with lace.

Then & Now

Protective paper: The earliest surviving objects made from papier-mache are two Chinese helmets created during the second century. They were painted with many coats of lacquer in order to strengthen them for protection in battle.

ARTIST'S CHOICE!

Finishing: Here are three options for how to "glaze" or seal your sculpture and give it a shiny surface:

★ Paint with a mixture of equal parts white glue and water.

★ Paint small pieces with clear nail polish.

★ Have a grown-up help you apply clear acrylic sealer.

Art Smart

★ Work outdoors. Papier-mache is as messy as it is fun. Fresh air also helps the pieces dry faster.

★ Clean-up is easier while the paste is wet, so wipe off paste spills before they dry. Protect work areas with newspaper.

★ Make just the amount of paste you need for your projects. Even when stored in the refrigerator, the paste starts to spoil after a few days.

★ OUTRAGEOUS HEADGEAR ★

Make outrageous headgear using mash (see page 100). Mash can be molded any way you like and dried mash is very lightweight, so it's the perfect concoction for making heady stuff. Check out the characters in a Dr. Seuss book for ideas, or look in a book about prehistoric creatures or a book about birds for inspiration. Then let your own imagination take flight.

WHAT YOU NEED

Mash (see page 100)

Bowl

Petroleum jelly

Pencil

Blunt knife

Decorating and finishing materials (page 102)

Yarn

WHAT YOU DO

1 Find a bowl that fits on your head like a cap. (The papier-mache cap will end up slightly larger.) Coat the outside surface of the bowl with petroleum jelly so that the mash won't stick.

2 Prepare the mash, and press it over the entire surface of the bowl. Use a pencil point to make a stringing hole in each side of the cap. Let the mash dry.

3 When the mash cap is completely dry, pry it gently from the base bowl with a blunt knife. You now have a basic cap to decorate.

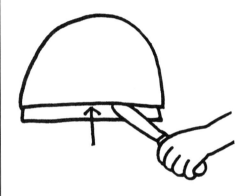

4 Use globs of mash to mold horns, ears, beaks, bumps, or any strange forms on top of the cap. You may need to tape on forms for support structures if you want large appendages growing out of your cap (see page 105 for form ideas).

5 Use any of the decorating ideas (see page 102) to add color, texture, detail, and whimsy to your headgear.

6 Tie about 2 feet (60 cm) of yarn in each stringing hole. Tie the headgear on your head and wear proudly.

★ TALKING HEADS ★

Mash is wonderful for making puppet heads on sticks. And because it's so easy to mold, you can create a unique look for each puppet. How will your puppet look — joyful, clever, or mean? Use mash to build up bushy eyebrows, puffy cheeks, a curled mustache, pointy chin, or wide, smiling lips. The personality you create for your puppet is what will make it special.

1 Mold a glob of mash into a simple head shape. Give the face a special personality.

2 Once the head is close to the way you want it, insert a dowel, about 14 inches (35 cm) long, into the neck. Press the mash tightly around the stick. Reshape the head and face.

3 Check on the puppet as it dries. You may need to add more mash where the stick comes out of the head. You can still change the nose or other features by adding more mash, even after the head is dry.

4 Once dry, turn puppet on its side and add mash to the back of the head to make it round. Work on a flat surface or set the stick in a plastic soda bottle weighted with dry rice or sand.

5 Let the back side dry. See pages 102 for decorative and finishing ideas to complete your puppet. Use white glue to attach yarn hair, button eyes, or a cloth hat. Or, add paint to the special puppet personality you formed.

HEADIN' OUT

What do astronauts, football players, and firefighters have in common? They all rely on specialized headgear. While the astronaut's head-gear provides precious oxygen, the football player's helmet guards the head from injury. Specially shaped helmets help water and burning debris slide right off firefighters' heads. Even a farmer's straw hat is specially designed.

The brim provides sun protection, while the cone-shaped crown forms a vented air space to let the air circulate.

People, such as the knights in medieval times, first wore headgear for protection, but they just couldn't resist adding creative touches here and there. Steel helmets from China, over two thousand years old, have been found inlaid with gold and jewels.

KID BIZ

Make many puppet personalities to sell at a craft fair. Create heads that match the theme of the fair. Let's say your town holds a Renaissance Fair. Make several queens, kings, knights, jesters, and dragons. You might even dress up as a knight or damsel to attract customers. For a county fair, make animal heads or talking vegetables to sell.

Use plastic soda bottles to display your heads. Fill bottles part way with sand or rice so they don't topple over. Wrap and tape a different-colored sheet of paper around each bottle. Set them out in a colorful row. Include a few samples of Outrageous Headgear (see page 103) that match the fair theme. Adventurous customers can walk away with pig ears or look as if corn is growing from their heads! Split your profits with a donation to a good cause that interests you.

★ ROBOTS ★

Food packaging boxes and paper rolls make great robot shapes. Papier-mache strips are the perfect way to cover and hold the form together.

WHAT YOU DO

1 Use your imagination to make a robot form. Connect the pieces with masking tape.

2 Cover form completely with a layer of strips, overlaying them so there are no spaces. Cover with 4-6 layers. Be sure to let each layer dry overnight or for several hours before you apply the next.

3 Glue on bolts and washers, paint it bright colors, or use pieces of sea glass for robot lights, and small springs for appendages. Who knows what robots will really look like in the 21st century? Here's your chance to develop a prototype.

STAND UP AND BE COUNTED!

After you've created a sculpture, you'll want to display it for everyone to admire. Here are some simple ideas for making a stand you'll be proud to display:

★ Make a base from clay. Form it into any shape you want! The base can actually become part of the sculpture itself. Stick a bent hanger or wooden dowel into the clay, and then let base dry. Glue your sculpture to the stand, or tie on with small pieces of scrap wire.

★ Ask a restaurant to begin saving corks from wine bottles for you. Glue these together to create a stand for several small pieces of sculpture. Attach the sculpture to the base by sticking toothpicks or thin nails into the cork and into the base of your sculpture.

★ Create a stand from papier-mache. Cover a piece of wood, styrofoam, or aluminum foil with strips, or create a form from mash, and incorporate it right into your sculpture.

★ Turn to found objects for a creative and attractive base. Look for interesting rocks to glue your sculpture to (glue a piece of felt on the base of the rock to prevent scratches), twigs with a small "V" in them to prop in a container of soil (lean your sculpture against the "V"), or an interesting piece of wood.

MORE MASH

Here are two concoctions for moldable mash made from the recycled fibers of different paper products. Which mash do you like working with most?

★ TISSUE PAPER MASH ★

The tissue paper crumpled inside your new pair of sneakers can become a fish swimming at the end of your pencil! Tissue Paper Mash is great for making small works of art. You can also use it to add fine details to larger papier-mache creations.

Your mash will be a faded shade of the color tissue paper you make it from. White tissue is cleaner to work with and takes on color nicely.

WHAT YOU NEED

Several sheets of tissue paper

Liquid starch

WHAT YOU DO

1 Tear tissue paper into small pieces. Add enough starch to wet the paper.

2 Press the concoction into a firm glob. Squeeze out the excess starch.

3 Squeeze the glob until it feels like a workable dough.

4 Store in an airtight container.

PENCIL TOPPERS

Put an interesting character at the tip of your pencil to cheer you on while you do your homework! The mash is very lightweight when dry, so the character will not interfere with your writing as it peers at your work.

WHAT YOU DO

1 Mold a small glob of Tissue Paper Mash into a simple head shape. The mash is lumpy so it's a little tricky to work with.

2 Once the shape is close to the way you want it, insert a pencil into the neck. Remold the head to fit onto the pencil.

3 Stick pencil in the backside of an empty egg carton to dry. (This also makes a good display rack if you decide to sell them.)

4 Use felt-tip markers to decorate, or leave the natural color of the tissue paper. Dip the markers in water to help the color flow better over the rough paper surface.

ARTIST'S CHOICE!

Tissue Paper Mash can also be made with:

★ Paper napkins

★ Paper towels

★ Toilet paper

★ Facial tissue

ART SMART

You can also mold a Pencil Topper onto the rounded end of a nonspring-type wooden clothespin or doll pin. Make animal shapes, too. Clip your characters onto un-likely spots around the house — curtains, hand towels, cloth napkins, or school papers.

★ CREPE PAPER MASH ★

When the party's over and you've torn down those crepe paper streamers, you can still have fun! Mold those streamers into something new and different.

WHAT YOU NEED

1 roll of crepe paper

Water

1/2 cup (125 ml) flour

1/4 cup (75 ml) salt

WHAT YOU DO

1 Tear crepe paper into small pieces and soak in a bowl of water overnight.

2 Drain and squeeze most of the water from the pulp. Measure 1 packed cup (250 ml) of crepe paper pulp into the mixing bowl.

3 Add flour and salt. Press the mixture into a firm glob.

4 Knead the glob until it feels like a workable dough.

5 Store in an airtight container.

★ CREPE PAPER POTTERY ★

Make a pretty set of bowls, each in a different color of crepe paper. Crepe Paper Mash is a concoction that likes to cling together, almost like wet cloth. It's great for draping over forms (see Drape-a-Slab, page 117). Mold it around a tin can or a glass jar for a fresh flower vase, or a paper cup to make a vase for dried flowers. The mash's color will be a lighter version of the original crepe paper. It dries amazingly strong and can be decorated and sealed the same way as a papier-mache sculpture (see page 102). Display your creation for everyone to admire, or give it as a gift for someone else to treasure!

EARTHWORKS

As you know, soil is essential to life, for how else would plants grow to feed humans and animals? Did you ever think that soil is essential to many art forms? The soil beneath our feet is the source of some the world's oldest and most amazing pottery, paintings, and architecture. The concoctions in this section will help you discover why artists value substances as ordinary as soil and sand for their creations.

ALL OF A KIND

Soils and sands vary greatly from one location to another. The soil in a rain forest is surprisingly shallow; a thin layer sits on top of hard bedrock. You'll often find deep, rich soils in the flat areas alongside rivers. River beds (bottoms) are covered with fine mineral particles called *silt*. When rivers flood, the silt is brought up and left alongside the river to make the perfect soil for growing — and creating. Ancient Egyptian potters used this special soil alongside the Nile River to make their beautiful pottery.

Sand can provide an artist with a palette full of colors. Most tan sand is made of quartz rock, ground to fine particles over many, many years' time. In areas of volcanic activity, dark minerals make sand a rich black color. The beautiful white sands of New Mexico are almost pure gypsum. Navajo artists collect special colors of sand for their sand-painting ceremonies.

MUDWORKS

Here's your chance to muck around in marvelous mud! Just tell a grown-up that you want to be a soils specialist when you grow up, and you need to investigate all that soil can do. There's lots to learn about dirt — and lots of wonderful things to do with it!

★ MUD FOSSILS ★

WHAT YOU NEED

Dirt

Water

Shovel

WHAT YOU DO

1 Check with a grown-up for a place where it's okay to dig a hole in the dirt. Stay away from lawns and gardens.

2 Dig a hole. Add a little water — not so much that it is soupy. Use your shovel or a stick to stir the water and dirt together. The mixture should look like brown mashed potatoes.

3 Scoop up some of the wet dirt in your hands.

4 Mold as you like. Don't expect to be able to make any shape. The dirt will probably crumble. Mud pies are the easiest to make. Just pat them between your hands.

5 Press your hand or object into the surface of the pie to make a print.

6 Let the imprint dry in the sun.

ARTIST'S CHOICE!

This is a little tricky, but worth doing if you want to make an authentic-looking fossil. Stick a shell, thick leaf, or other small object in the center of your pie. Let the pie dry completely. Then, gently break open the pie. Remove the object. You should see its impression in both halves of the pie.

WHAT HAS NO EYES. . .

breaths through its skin, eats soil — and, if you gather every one of them on earth, weighs ten times the total weight of the entire human population? The amazing earthworm! Earthworms make wonderful soil for growing plants. A gardenful of earthworms passes tons of soil through their bodies. They drag humus (decaying plants) into their burrows. They bring air and water to plant roots as they tunnel around. Earthworm manure, called worm *casts*, contains lime that makes a rich soil for plants. Are earthworms the world's hardest working creature? Maybe so — and very helpful, too.

Then & Now

Being resourceful: Imagine you are an artist living many thousands of years ago. You look for different colors in soft rocks and soil, and then grind them to a fine powder using a bone on a stone. You mix this powder with animal fat. Now, with this concoction, you paint a picture on the cave wall of the animals you hunt. You add spears near the animal to bring good luck on the hunt. Brushes might be animal hairs tied onto twigs or bones. Or, you might use pads of fur, or moss, or your fingers to apply your paints. Well, guess what? That is exactly how artists so very long ago used to create their concoctions and their works of art!

★ MUD PAINTS ★

Try an art and an artist's concoction that's 30,000 years old! Mix your own soil powder with cooking oil instead of animal fat. Try painting a picture on a flat rock instead of a cave wall. Use your fingers, a stick, or a leaf for a paintbrush.

WHAT YOU NEED

Dirt

Cooking oil or water

Shovel or spoon

Newspaper

Sieve and pie plate

Small stick

Flat rock

WHAT YOU DO

1 Find an area of clean dirt. Put a shovelful in a can.

2 If the soil is perfectly dry, skip to step 4. If the soil is at all moist, set it out on some newspaper in the sun. Let it dry thoroughly.

3 You now have a dry clump of soil. Remove all twigs and rocks you see. Smash the clump into powder using a rock or hammer.

4 Use a sieve to sift the powder onto a pie plate. Throw away pebbles and rock chips. The pie plate now holds clean dirt for paint powder.

5 Add some cooking oil, and stir the dirt and oil together. The mixture should look like heavy cream.

6 Use fingers, a leaf, or stick to paint the mud onto a flat rock, or some paper. Make several colors of paint by using different kinds of soil (red clay soil is nice if you can find some).

SWAMPY BLACK

The Senufo tribe of the Ivory Coast in Africa knows just where to go for a special black dye — to the local swamp. They use the deep black mud found there to make designs on cloth. They paint crocodiles, turtles, and other animals of their coastal home, and then wear the decorated cloth when they hunt. The bold pattern makes the hunter hard to see among the thick jungle plants. The animal symbols are believed to bring good luck and a big catch.

Art Smart

The oil in Mud Paint causes the image to spread out and blur. This works well for paintings of rainbows and sunsets, or shimmering water scenes like the Impressionists painted. If you want to do more clearly outlined images, then substitute water for the oil in the Mud Paint concoction. Like every good artist, change the concoction to suit your needs.

NATURAL CLAY

It may not be the best and you may have to dig deeply —but it's fun to try "mining" clay right from your own backyard. Look for soft, claylike material. Depending on where you look, clay might be brown, greenish, red, yellow, black, gray, or even white. In some areas, natural clay is plentiful. In other areas it's very difficult to find. Ask folks who like to garden about the soil in your area.

WHAT MAKES CLAY SO MOLDABLE?

Clay is a special kind of soil. Its particles are extremely small. Some clay particles are one thousand times smaller than the particles of sandy soil. Each tiny particle can be coated with water. This helps the particles stick together. No wonder clay makes such a smooth molding substance.

★ EARTH'S CLAY ★

You may find a clay bed by digging beneath the surface in your own backyard. But the best places to search (with a grown-up only) are where the earth has been cut through where a highway has been made, a foundation excavated, a trench has been dug, or alongside a creek or river. Please don't go off to these places without a grown-up.

What may look like a rock might actually be dried clay. Break off a chunk to see if it holds its shape (rock) or crumbles (dried clay). Test different soil samples. Add a little water to a small chunk. See if you can roll it into a ball or snake. If it holds together, you've probably found clay.

WHAT YOU NEED

Clay bed

Water

Large coffee can

Shovel

Newspapers

Sieve or piece of screening

Bowl and old cloth

Airtight storage container

WHAT YOU DO

1 After you've found an area of clean clay soil, start digging. Fill a large coffee can with some clean, clayey soil.

2 If your soil is at all moist, set it out on some newspaper in the sun. Let it dry out thoroughly.

3 Then, remove all twigs and rocks from the dry clumps of soil. Smash the clumps into powder using a rock or hammer.

4 Using a sieve, sift the powder back into the coffee can. Throw away pebbles and rock chips. The coffee can should now be partially filled with a beautiful flourlike clay powder.

5 Cover the clay powder completely with water. Add more water as the water soaks in, using your hands to break up lumps.

6 Let the creamy mixture sit overnight.

7 The next day, pour off the extra water that hasn't soaked into the clay. Then, line a large bowl with an old cloth. Pour the very wet clay into the bowl. (The cloth helps absorb some of the extra water from the clay.) Let the clay dry out.

8 When the clay feels soft enough to handle easily, it's ready to use. Store it moist in an airtight container.

Art Smart

★ Is your clay too floppy? Add small amounts of sand to help it hold its shape. Too sandy? Sorry, you're out of luck. Start again with soil from a new location.

★ Clay is nicest after it has set for a while.

★ In a hurry? Add a little water to the clay powder you made in step 4, page 115. Even though the clay hasn't reached its prime, you can start molding!

★ Remove all air bubbles from the clay before you work with it. Do this by slamming chunks of clay, many times, against your work surface. Potters call this *wedging*. Check the clay by cutting it in half with a piece of wire stretched tightly between your two hands. Look at the inside of the clay. It should be bubble-free.

★ PERFECT POTS ★

The discovery of pottery was very important to ancient people. They needed pots to store and cook their food. Early pots were sometimes decorated by engraving with a stick on the pot before it dried. You can make pots in the same way they've been made for thousands of years. Work small; homemade clays are usually not strong enough to support large constructions.

WHAT YOU NEED

Earth's Clay

WHAT YOU DO

Pinch-a-pot: Form a ball. Push your thumbs into the center of the ball. Use your fingers to build up the sides from the center, thinning the walls of the pot evenly. Smooth the inside and outside of the pot with wet fingers. Keep working the shape until it looks like a pot.

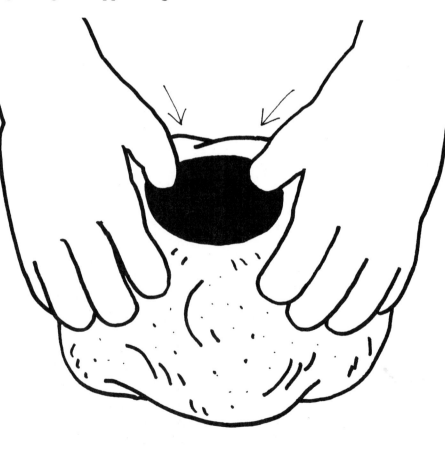

Coil-a-pot: Make several snakes (see Molding, page 50). Cover them with a damp cloth. Use one to make a tight coil. Use wet fingers to fill in any spaces. This will be the base of the pot. Now build up the walls. Place a coil around the edge of the base. Wet the coil where you want it to stick to the base and stick to the next coil. Keep adding coils until the pot is as tall as you want it to be.

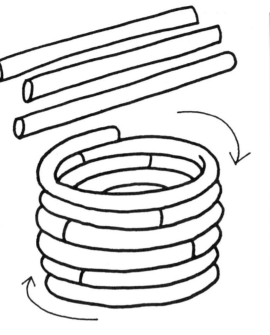

Geometric constructions: Construct an open cube pot. Roll out a slab. Use a dull knife or square cookie cutter to cut 5 small squares, all the same size. Use one square as the base. Attach the other four as walls. Use wet fingers to moisten the edges of the slabs and gently press them together. Use wet fingers to smooth seams and gently mold the cube to the desired shape. You can also make rectangular constructions. You can attach one slab around an oval or round base.

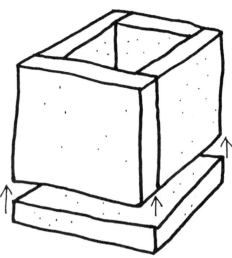

Drape-a-slab: Make a slab (see Molding, page 50). Drape the outside surface of a small bowl with a wet cloth. This will keep the clay from sticking to the bowl. Drape the slab over the cloth. Gently mold the slab around the bowl. When the slab is dry, remove the bowl. You can also use the inside of the bowl as the surface to lay the slab on top of. Or, drape irregular-shaped slabs over smooth, clean rocks for unusual-shaped bowls.

Creature pots: Some of the earliest cups, pots, and vessels were made to look like animals. With a little extra pinching, you can pinch a pot to look like a bird or other creature. Add clay on the front of the pot to make the neck and head. Add clay on the back to form the tail. Make wings flat against the side. Your bird-in-the-hand is also a pot!

ARTIST'S CHOICE!

Let your craft dry in the open air.

Long ago people discovered that if they fired their pottery, the pieces were stronger, could hold liquid, and could be used for cooking. If you are interested in learning to fire and glaze your pieces, you'll need special instructions. Ask your art teacher, a potter, or a teacher at a craft school for help.

KID BIZ

Package chunks of local clay you've mined and prepared. Name the clay for the area it comes from, such as *Shasta Red* or *Grass Valley Gray*. Put the clay in plastic bags. Tag each one with an artistic Custom-Designed Sticker (see page 76). You can also make art works from local clay. Again, give each piece a special name tag, "This piece is made especially for you from Ashland Brown Clay." Both your art works and the raw clay can be good sellers at a craft fair.

Pottery made from clay soil in a friend's backyard makes a very special gift for that friend.

YOU BE THE ARCHAEOLOGIST!

You've been digging all day without much luck. Suddenly you discover two fragments of pottery. "These must be 7000 years old!" You inspect them carefully and notice three important things:

1 They are both black.

2 One piece is very round, curving to the side and across the bottom.

3 A basketlike print covers the other.

"How were these pots made?" Here's how other archaeologists have put the clues together. Early pots were black because they were thrown into bonfires to harden. Most likely a clay pot accidentally fell into the fire. People then discovered that a baked pot became hard, strong, waterproof, and useful for cooking. First pots had rounded bottoms because they were probably molded around stones or gourds like the Drape-a-slab pots on page 117. Pot fragments are often covered with basketlike prints because many early pots were made from baskets. People covered baskets with clay so that small seeds would not fall through the basket holes.

Pottery is very special to archaeologists. Because pottery is hard and strong, it is often the only record left of many ancient peoples.

INSIDE DIRT

Pick up a lump of soil and let it squish between your fingers. It's amazing to think that soft soil was once hard rock. Rock was softened by *weathering* — rain and wind breaking it into smaller and smaller pieces. That lump of soil is also made up of tiny bits of dead plants and animals. These are called *humus* or *organic matter*.

Do you want to take a close look at what the soil around your home is made of? Use water to separate out the different soil particles and see.

1 Put a soil sample in a jar.

2 Add enough water to almost fill the jar.

3 Shake; then let the jar stand.

4 Observe. Organic matter (dead plants and animals) will float to the top. Mineral particles (tiny pieces of rock) will sink.

5 Try this experiment with soil samples from several locations. Compare what you see in each jar.

Art Smart

Even if you don't have access to a natural clay bed, you can still make pots. Just use the dough you like best from Hands-On Doughs, pages 45–108.

★ ADOBE BRICKS ★

Adobe means clay in Spanish, and that's exactly what these bricks are made of. If you like getting into squishy mud, adobe brick-making is for you!

WHAT YOU NEED

Soil

Water

Dry grass clippings or straw (ask at a local nursery)

Hand shovel

Milk carton

Scissors

Blunt knife

WHAT YOU DO

1 Dig a small hole away from lawns and other plants. Put some of the loose dirt back into the hole. Add a handful of dry grass clippings. Add enough water to make the soil moldable.

2 Start working the mixture with your hands. Your goal is to make an even blend of dirt, straw, and water — no wet spots, no dry spots. Add more water or more soil if needed. The adobe is ready when it's stiff enough to stand up and wet enough to mold.

3 To make a brick mold, ask a grown-up to help you cut out opposite sides of a milk carton. Sprinkle a clear spot of ground with straw where you will dry the brick. Set the mold on top.

4 Fill the mold right to the top with tightly packed adobe. Fill the corners first, then the side edges, then the center. Let set for a few moments.

5 Use a dull knife to cut between the adobe and the edge of the mold. Carefully lift the mold and leave the brick standing. Do not move the brick until it is dry. Make more bricks in different spots.

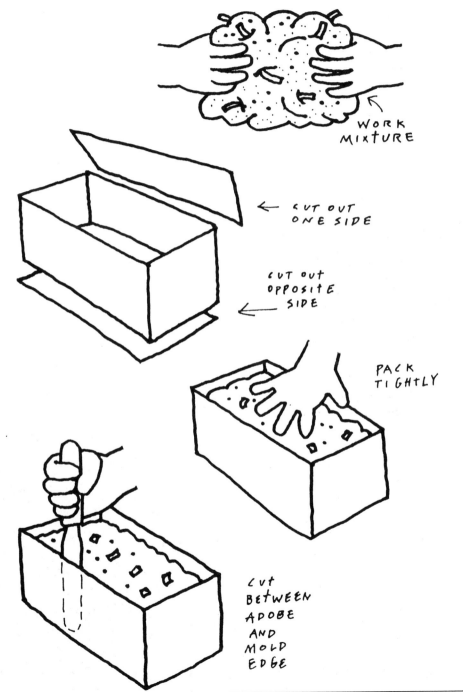

WORK MIXTURE

← CUT OUT ONE SIDE

CUT OUT OPPOSITE SIDE ←

PACK TIGHTLY

CUT BETWEEN ADOBE AND MOLD EDGE

ARTIST'S CHOICE!

For cylindrical bricks, use a coffee can with the top and bottom ends removed as a mold.

Make bricks the way they've been made around the world and for centuries — invite some friends to help. With grown-up permission, dig a hole about three feet (90 cm) across, large enough to hold about three stomping kids. Shovel clean clay soil into the hole, about four inches (10 cm) deep. Avoid rocks and sticks. They hurt bare feet! Sprinkle pieces of short straw on top. Add enough water to make the soil moldable. Start stomping with one to three bare-foot kids moving in a circle in the hole. Ask a grown-up to help you make a larger mold from wood. Continue with steps three through five. Try building a wall with your bricks. Use wet adobe for mortar.

WHERE IN THE WORLD?

For thousands of years, and all over the world, people have used the soil beneath their feet to build their homes. Mud and chopped straw are mixed. The mixture is packed into a wooden mold. The shaped mud dries in the sun. Bricks are stacked to build walls.

Bricks will dissolve in the rain, so builders cover the outside walls with a thick layer of the same mixture of mud and straw. The *slurry* is spread thick enough to protect the bricks. The idea is for the rain to dissolve the slurry and not the bricks. Every year, after the rainy season, slurry must be spread on the walls again to protect the bricks.

SAND ART

Sand has fascinated people since the beginning of time. Whether you are playing in a sandbox, making a sand painting from a container of sand you brought home from the beach, or joining artists of all ages in a sand castle contest on the shore, you are sure to discover the appeal of nature's very own wonderful concoction.

CHRISTO'S WAY

Margaret Wolfe Hungerford once said that "beauty is in the eye of the beholder," and that's certainly true of art. One controversial artist named Christo created a 20-foot (6 m) fence that spanned 24 miles (nearly 40 km). Guess what he named his creation? You guessed it, *Running Fence*.

You can do just as Christo did and make the most wonderful artistic creations using the area where you live as a medium, instead of using paper or clay. Create a beach painting with shells and seaweed or stack up a pile of rocks into a special formation. Or, collect roadside debris on Green-Up Day and make a work of art from your findings. The sky's the limit!

SANDSCAPES

WHAT YOU NEED

Sand

Water

Hand shovel

Molds: Buckets, cans, plastic soda bottle cut in half (the neck makes an interesting added shape), gelatin molds, bundt cake pan, plastic flower pots, yogurt containers, and margarine tubs

Sand shapers (see Art Smart), block of wood

Decorations: beachcombing finds

The fun of creating sandscapes is that your imagination is your only limit. One of the best things about creating a sandscape is that you'll meet lots of people of all ages at the beach — everyone will want to join in the fun. Be sure to take pictures of your finished creations before the tide comes in.

WHAT YOU DO

1 The best place to build a sand castle or a sandscape is near the shore. Look for sand that is moist, but not too gloppy. You can also build in a sandbox, adding just the right amount of water to hold the sand together.

2 Pack sand firmly with your hands as you build up or tunnel down.

3 If you are using a mold, pack the sand firmly. Quickly turn the mold upside down. Or, skip the "upside-down" step by using a can with both the bottom and top cut out. Simply pack with sand and gently lift off the mold.

4 Use a block of wood to create flat surfaces. Just run the wood along the top edge of a wall.

5 Press decorations into the sand. Whatever you find beachcombing will add interest to your sandscape.

Make a sand shaper: Use sand shapers to cut a ridge, or square off a sand wall. Ask a grown-up to help you cut a semicircle shape or a corner shape from the plastic lid of a large yogurt container or the side of a plastic gallon milk jug. Run the sand shaper along the sand mound you want shaped.

ARTIST'S CHOICE!

Sand sculpture: You can mold moist sand into any interesting shape, not just a castle. Start by pressing the sand together into mounds. You'll get ideas as you work with the sand, but here are some to get you started:

Nature's own: Fish, sea turtles, dolphins, the sun

Imaginary creatures: Dinosaurs, monsters, robots

Sunbathers: Make life-size people. Give your sand friends real sunglasses, flippers, a newspaper, and some soda pop.

★ CASTLE FOR KEEPS ★

Although you can't bring your sand castle home from the beach, you can bring home a bucketful of sand. Here's a concoction that you can make into a small castle that's crumble-proof.

WHAT YOU NEED

2 cups (500 ml) sand

1 cup (250 ml) cornstarch

1 cup (250 ml) water

Newspaper

WHAT YOU DO

1 Mix sand, cornstarch, and water in an old pot.

2 Ask a grown-up to help you cook the mixture over low heat. Stir all the time.

3 When the mixture thickens, remove from stove and let it cool.

4 Turn it out on newspaper. Mold into a castle or any simple shape you like.

NATURE'S SANDY MASTERPIECE

Nature creates sand art all on her own in the wonderful sand dunes. These fantastic formations are created when winds blow sand around into beautiful formations and mounds. If the mound is large enough, it will attract more sand and can actually become quite enormous — as tall as a major hillside!

Often tall grasses — called dune grass — grow atop the large dunes. Dune grass helps protect the delicate dunes from erosion by the wind and water. But these spectacular dunes are still very fragile. Be sure never to walk or picnic on dunes. Just enjoy nature's art work from afar.

★ COLORED SAND OR RICE ★

The Navajo Indians of southwestern United States made sacred designs by trickling sand between their fingers. The colored sands they used were from nature: sandstone for red and brown, charcoal for black, and limestone for white. You can look for and save different-colored sands. Or, color your own. You can use sand, salt, or rice for these projects.

WHAT YOU NEED

For each color:

½ cup (125 ml) clean, sifted sand or rice

¼ cup (50 ml) alcohol or water

Food coloring

Bucket and sieve

Container with lid for each color

Newspaper

WHAT YOU DO

1 First sift and clean the sand. Use a sieve to sift fine grains of sand into a bucket. Now pour water into the bucket to clean the sand. Carefully drain the water through the sieve. Dump sand back into the bucket. Repeat until the water runs out clear. For rice, skip this cleaning step and start with step 2.

2 Mix water and several drops of food coloring in the jar. Add more coloring for a deeper color. Or, ask a grown-up to help you use alcohol (it dries faster than water). Add the sand.

3 Stir the mixture, or screw on the lid and shake the container, until the sand is evenly colored.

4 Let the sand sit in the colored water for at least 15 minutes (about 5 minutes for rice). Then, carefully pour out the extra water using a sieve.

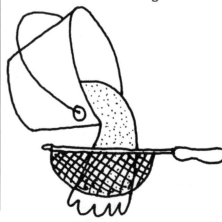

5 Spread sand out to dry on newspaper. Move it around from time to time so that all particles can dry. When dry, pour the sand back into the container.

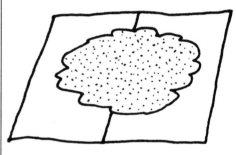

6 Repeat these steps for each color. While rice and salt absorb food coloring very well, sand does not. Your sand color will be subtle while rice and salt colors are more intense.

★ COLORED SALT ★

Using chalk

WHAT YOU NEED

For each color:

Salt

Colored sidewalk chalk

Sheet of paper

Container with a lid

WHAT YOU DO

1 Pour salt on the paper.

2 Rub chalk over the salt. The more you rub, the deeper the color of the salt.

3 Carefully pour colored salt into the container.

4 Store salt in the container.

5 Repeat these steps for each color.

Using food coloring

WHAT YOU NEED

For each color:

1/2 cup (125 ml) salt

Food coloring

Container with a lid

WHAT YOU DO

1 Pour salt into the container. Add several drops of food coloring.

2 Stir until the salt is evenly colored. The more coloring you add, the deeper the color of the salt.

3 Set the open container in a warm, dry place. Let the salt dry by stirring damp salt to the top from time to time.

4 Store dry salt in the jar.

5 Repeat these steps for each color.

WHAT IN THE WORLD?

Sand is simply itty-bitty, incredibly tiny . . . rock. The solid rock surfaces of the earth have been breaking up for millions of years. While some rock particles become soil (see Inside Dirt, page 120), other super-gritty particles remain sand. Why do you think some sand is rough on your feet and other sand is as soft and smooth as powder?

Take a look at a pinch of sand under a magnifying glass. Each grain has a story. The round, smooth grains were probably smoothed against an ocean shore. Or, maybe they've traveled long and far. The grains with sharp edges are young by sand standards. They've probably broken off from rock more recently and haven't had a chance to become smooth.

★ SAND PAINTING ★

Create designs that look like Navajo symbols. Find examples in an encyclopedia or *The Kids' Multicultural Art Book*, by A. Terzian. Or sand-paint original designs: wildlife, landscapes, portraits, your name, or geometric shapes.

WHAT YOU NEED

2 or more colors of sand

White glue

Water

Heavy drawing paper or sandpaper

Cookie sheet or tray

Paintbrush

WHAT YOU DO

1 Mix a spoonful of glue and a spoonful of water together in a cup.

2 Use a pencil to lightly draw your design on the paper. Set the paper in the tray. Think about how the colored sand will fill the different areas.

3 Use the paintbrush to paint all areas where you want one color of sand to stick.

4 Use a spoon or your fingers to sprinkle the sand over the glue. Let sand set for a few moments.

5 Gently turn the paper over the tray and tap to let the extra sand fall off.

6 Set the paper aside. Pour the extra sand in the tray back into the jar of colored sand.

7 Continue painting the glue, sprinkling the sand, and turning the paper over for each color until your sand painting is complete.

IIKAY

Art Smart

★ Glue the colors, starting with the lightest color first and finishing with the darkest color.

★ Make sure every bit of glue is covered with sand. Sprinkle on plenty. You'll be tapping off the extra sand.

★ Give each color about ten minutes to set before moving on to the next.

Iikay, the Navajo word for sand painting, means "where the gods come and go." Sand painting was used by the Navajos to bring the gods to their very special healing ceremonies.

Sometimes as many as six men would work for four hours to make a beautiful painting in the sand. Some paintings were as large as 35 feet (10.5 m) across. Sand paintings showed legends of spirits who could cure the sick. Symbols of nature, such as mountains, thunder, lightning, plants, and animals were painted to represent the gods. The sick person sat in the center of the painting, and singers chanted prayers. The painting was destroyed at the end of the ceremony; otherwise, it was believed it would bring bad luck.

ARTIST'S CHOICE!

Paint and sprinkle freely without planning a pencil design. Decide where you want colors as you go.

- - - - - - - - - - - -

Sand paint with colored sand, salt, rice, or all three. Check out different grains such as wheat berries, brown rice, or barley for different colors and textures.

- - - - - - - - - - - -

Sand paint on sandpaper to make your art work look like it's sitting on desert sand.

- - - - - - - - - - - -

Cut cardboard or cardboard-backed sandpaper into small shapes. Sand paint. Seal with clear acrylic sealer. Stick a magnet on back to display.

★ LAYERED SAND JAR ★

Make a sedimentary rock model. The layers of colored sand create a beautiful display, as well as give you an idea how sedimentary rock is formed.

WHAT YOU NEED

A variety of colored sands

Nicely shaped clear jar with a lid

Funnel

WHAT YOU DO

1 Spoon a layer of colored sand into the jar. Or, pour the sand through a funnel into the jar. Gently tap the jar to make the sand level.

2 Continue adding layers of different-colored sands until you reach the top.

3 Screw the lid on the jar.

ARTIST'S CHOICE!

Use colored salt or rice.

- - - - - - - - - -

Use any colors in any order.

- - - - - - - - - -

Repeat colors in a certain order. Make a rainbow jar by using colors in this order: red, orange, yellow, green, blue, indigo, violet.

- - - - - - - - - -

Vary the widths of the layers.

- - - - - - - - - -

Slope the layers.

- - - - - - - - - -

Push one color into another. Push a long, thin stick along the edge of the glass through all layers of sand. When you carefully pull the stick out, sand from one layer will be drawn into the layer beneath it. Continue pushing colors all around the jar. The trick is to get a flow of color without mixing it so much that you can't distinguish the layers.

WHAT'S SEDIMENTARY?

Earth's ancient rocks are several million years old. But rocks don't last forever. They keep changing. Rain, wind, freezing, and thawing erode (break up) rocks at the earth's surface. This broken down material is called *sediment*. Sediment can be found at the bottom of the sea or a river. Layers and layers of rock particles build up on top of each other. The layers are pressed together to make new rock called sedimentary rock. Look at pictures of the Grand Canyon for a spectacular example of layered red sandstone and limestone.

CONCOCTION COMBOS

For twice the fun, why not combine concoctions? Paint + paste + dough = something wonderfully new and totally different from the concoction you started with.

SPECIAL PAPERS

What can you do with all those beautiful special papers you've made? Lots! Use them to wrap gifts. Fold small pieces in half to make greeting cards. Or, try one of the many projects in this section.

TOUGH COATING

In order to use your special papers in a variety of ways — or display them without the edges curling up — you may want to increase their durability in one of the following ways:

Paper-backed: Select a solid-colored sheet of paper the same size as the special paper. Coat the solid sheet with a thin layer of paper paste. Gently rub and press the sheets together with your hands, and let dry.

Cardboard-backed: Use lightweight cardboard from a used cereal box or cracker box. Paste the special paper onto the printed side of cardboard as described for paper-backing.

Vinyl-covered: If the paint on the special paper feels gritty, you may wish to cover it with clear, adhesive-backed, vinyl shelf paper. This will make the special paper very durable; you can even use it as a place mat.

Art Smart

Paper paste (see recipe page 77) works best for pasting paper to paper or paper to uncoated cardboard. If the cardboard has a slick (coated) surface, you will need to use rubber cement or white glue. White glue works best for sticking paper to the metal surface of a can.

★ COVER-UPS ★

Humble cans and plain boxes become part of elegant desk sets when covered with special paper. Transform an ordinary picture frame into a one-of-a-kind home decoration.

WHAT YOU NEED

Paper paste, page 77–78

White glue

Special paper

Item to be covered

WHAT YOU DO

Boxes: Trace the shape of the panels you wish to cover onto the back of a sheet of special paper. Cut out and paste in place. Small boxes can be used as part of a desk set to hold paper clips or rubber bands. Larger boxes can hold special stationery (page 134).

Cans: Measure the height and perimeter (distance around the circle) of a can. Add about one inch (2.5 cm) to the perimeter measurement for overlap. (An easy way to do this is to wrap a piece of scrap paper around the can and then cut it to fit. Use as a template.) Draw a rectangle onto the back of a sheet of special paper. Cut out and paste in place on the can. Use rubber bands to hold the paper in place while the glue dries.

Picture frame: Buy a matboard frame from an art supply store. Trace its shape onto special paper. Cut out the shape and paste into place on top of the matboard.

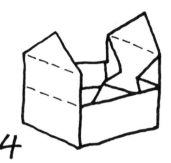

Can't find that special box? Make your own. Fold two squares of special paper as shown to make a unique box and lid.

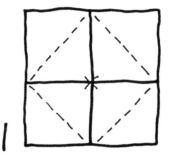

1 FOLD A SQUARE PIECE OF PAPER INTO QUARTERS. UNFOLD. FOLD EACH OUTER CORNER TO THE CENTER POINT.

2 ADD CREASE LINES EQUIDISTANT FROM OUTER EDGES.

3 UNFOLD OPPOSITE ENDS.

4 BRING UP SIDES ON FOLD LINES. BRING UP ENDS AND FOLD SO THAT THEY MEET IN THE CENTER.

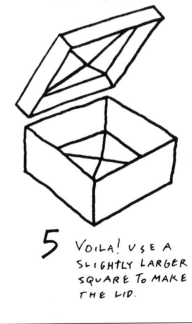

5 VOILA! USE A SLIGHTLY LARGER SQUARE TO MAKE THE LID.

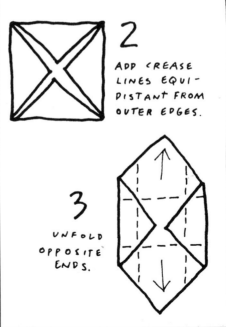

★ STUNNING STATIONERY ★

Combine special papers with Lick-It-Later Gum to make a special stationery set.

WHAT YOU NEED

Lick-It-Later Gum I or II (see page 74)

Special paper

White bond paper

Hole punch

WHAT YOU DO

Envelopes: Use the patterns shown on this page or carefully take apart an envelope and use it as a pattern. Trace the shape onto white or special paper. Fold your envelope along the same lines as the pattern envelope. Glue the edges that hold the envelope together now with paper paste or Lick-It-Later Gum. Paint Lick-It-Later Gum along the edges to be sealed later. Let it dry so the envelope can be sealed when used.

Writing paper: Make a decorative border on plain bond paper. Cut strips the length or width of the paper. Paste these strips along the side, top, or bottom edge of a sheet of writing paper.

Seals: Cut small, interesting shapes from special papers. Paint the back with Lick-It-Later Gum. These can be used to seal and decorate envelopes and stationery.

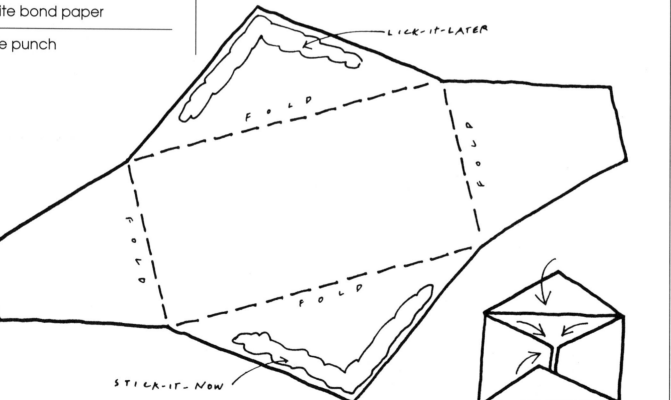

LICK-IT-LATER

FOLD

FOLD

FOLD

FOLD

FOLD

STICK-IT-NOW

Gift tags: Cut a 3" x 6" (7.5 cm x 15 cm) rectangle of special paper. Fold in half to form a card. Punch a hole in the top left corner. Thread thin ribbon or yarn through the hole.

Mini-message strips: Cut and fold as shown for an all-in-one message and envelope.

Bookmarks: Cut a long, thin rectangle from a sheet of cardboard-backed special paper. Punch a hole near the top. Thread it with ribbon or yarn. You can tie on a few beads for added pizzazz.

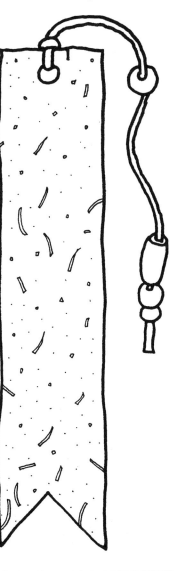

Stationery set: Package your sets in nicely decorated boxes (see page 133). Cover the box with the same special paper you used on the stationery. Tie a piece of ribbon or yarn around the writing paper and envelopes. Place the matching seals inside one of the envelopes. Place all items inside the special box. Stationery sets make lovely gifts or craft items to sell.

ARTIST'S CHOICE!

Something special: Decorate plain envelopes with bits of special paper to match the writing paper. Or, line the envelope with contrasting solid color or special paper. Trace a pattern of the inside back panel and back flap. Cut the lining about 1/2 inch (1 cm) smaller than the tracing. Paste it in place before folding the envelope.

BEAUTIFUL BOOKS

Use special papers to make unique photo albums, sketch books, or journals.

★ ACCORDION BOOK ★

Here's the perfect little book for recording words of wisdom or a special poem.

WHAT YOU NEED

2 square pieces of card-board the same size

2 scraps of special paper

Ribbon (long enough to wrap around the cardboard and tie into a bow)

One strip of blank paper

Paper paste (page 77)

Scissors and tape

WHAT YOU DO

1 Ribbon keeps your book closed. Hold it in place by taping the middle of the ribbon to the middle of one of the cardboard squares.

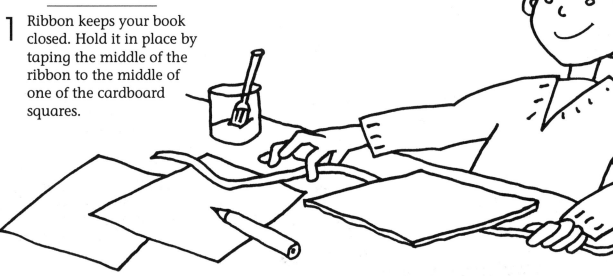

2 Cover each cardboard square with special paper. The paper will hold down the ribbon on one of the squares. These covered cardboard squares are the book covers. (You can also paste special paper on the inside of the covers if you like.)

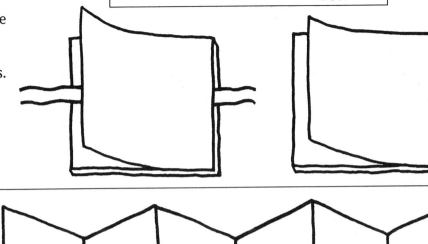

3 Accordion-fold a strip of paper to make the inside connected pages. Make sure you have an even number of squares when you unfold the strip.

4 Paste the end squares of the strip to the inside and back book covers. Center the end squares so that the cardboard forms a border around them.

5 Refold the book. Wrap the ribbon around the book and tie in a bow to keep the book closed.

ARTIST'S CHOICE!

Make your accordion book any size.

- - - - - - - -

Use colored paper for the inside accordion-folded strip.

- - - - - - - -

Make the strip any length you like, so your book will have the number of pages you want. Just be sure you have an even number of folded squares.

- - - - - - - -

Fill the book with pictures, a story, a poem, words of wisdom, or whatever you like. Or, leave the book blank and give it as a gift for someone to write in or paste in dried flowers, stamps, or sticker collections.

RHYTHM & RHYME

Even before people could write, they made up poems and shared them with each other. Long ago people wrote ballads telling of important events. The rhythm and rhyme of the ballads helped make the words easier to remember, as ballads were passed from one storyteller to the next.

Some forms of poetry have very specific rules about the way they rhyme and the number of syllables within each line. But poems don't have to follow rules or even rhyme. You can write a poem describing a feeling, event, person, or thing just by selecting special descriptive words.

Try writing a descriptive poem about yourself. Start and end the poem with your name. List words that say something about who you are in the middle. Stack the words up and you have a poem! Write a poem about a friend, copy each word onto a page of an accordion book, illustrate each word, and you have a great gift for someone special.

Matt

Musical

Math whiz

Creative

Athletic

My friend

Matt

ARTIST'S CHOICE!

Try another binding method.

---

1. Cut two binding strips of cardboard the length of the book's spine by about 1 inch (2.5 cm) wide. Cover them with solid-colored paper.

---

2. Assemble the book by placing the binding strips on the left edges of the front and back covers. Use spring clips to hold everything together.

---

3. Measure and mark three or four holes on the binding strip. Place them half an inch (1 cm) from the left edge, centered within the length, and equally distanced from each other.

---

4. Use a hammer and nail to make the holes where marked, through all the layers of the book.

---

5. Thread a needle with a double strand of embroidery floss. Stitch through the holes.

★ COLLECTOR'S ALBUMS ★

Use special albums to save photographs and souvenirs, collections and drawings, poetry and pressed flowers — in fact, just about anything that you want to keep in a safe, organized place.

WHAT YOU NEED

2 sheets of 8½" x 11" (21 cm x 27.5 cm) cardboard-backed, vinyl-covered special paper

12 sheets of white, 8½" x 11" (21 cm x 27.5 cm) paper

Yarn

Hole punch

WHAT YOU DO

1 Punch two holes in the vinyl-covered front-cover sheet, half an inch (1 cm) from the left edge and 2 inches (5 cm) down from the top and bottom edges.

2 Use this cover sheet as a stencil for marking the location of the holes on the back cover and center sheets.

3 Punch holes in the back cover and center sheets.

4 Thread the yarn through the holes, going in and out a few times. Tie in a bow on the front cover.

1. PUNCH HOLES IN COVER

2. USE COVER AS STENCIL

3. PUNCH HOLES IN BACK AND CENTER SHEETS

4. THREAD YARN AND TIE BOW

MY ALBUM

★ NOTEPAD COVER ★

Make an inspiring cover for ordinary spiral-bound notebooks and sketch pads.

WHAT YOU NEED

Spiral notepad

Special paper

Solid-colored paper

Paper paste (page 77)

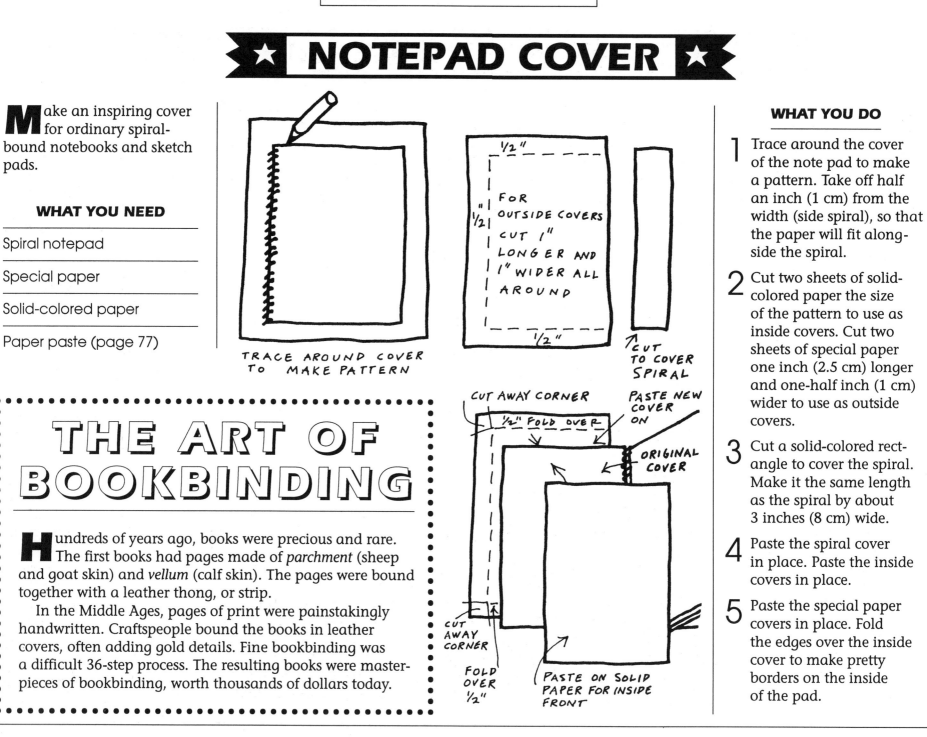

TRACE AROUND COVER TO MAKE PATTERN

1/2"
1/2" FOR OUTSIDE COVERS CUT 1" LONGER AND 1" WIDER ALL AROUND
1/2" 1/2"

CUT TO COVER SPIRAL

CUT AWAY CORNER
1/2" FOLD OVER
PASTE NEW COVER ON
ORIGINAL COVER
CUT AWAY CORNER
FOLD OVER 1/2"
PASTE ON SOLID PAPER FOR INSIDE FRONT

THE ART OF BOOKBINDING

Hundreds of years ago, books were precious and rare. The first books had pages made of *parchment* (sheep and goat skin) and *vellum* (calf skin). The pages were bound together with a leather thong, or strip.

In the Middle Ages, pages of print were painstakingly handwritten. Craftspeople bound the books in leather covers, often adding gold details. Fine bookbinding was a difficult 36-step process. The resulting books were masterpieces of bookbinding, worth thousands of dollars today.

WHAT YOU DO

1 Trace around the cover of the note pad to make a pattern. Take off half an inch (1 cm) from the width (side spiral), so that the paper will fit along-side the spiral.

2 Cut two sheets of solid-colored paper the size of the pattern to use as inside covers. Cut two sheets of special paper one inch (2.5 cm) longer and one-half inch (1 cm) wider to use as outside covers.

3 Cut a solid-colored rectangle to cover the spiral. Make it the same length as the spiral by about 3 inches (8 cm) wide.

4 Paste the spiral cover in place. Paste the inside covers in place.

5 Paste the special paper covers in place. Fold the edges over the inside cover to make pretty borders on the inside of the pad.

★ MOBILES AND ORNAMENTS ★

Make three-dimensional objects from special paper. When ornaments are complete, have a grown-up help you use a needle to poke a hanging thread through the top of the ornament. Hang individually or as part of a mobile from a coat hanger, dowel, or interesting branch.

WHAT YOU NEED

Special paper

Needle and thread

WHAT YOU DO

3-D object: Cut two identical shapes from the paper-backed special paper. Slit one shape up from the bottom and the other shape down from the top. Slide the two together for a three-dimensional shape. Try making the star on this page. Then make any shapes you choose in three dimensions.

Shape within a shape: Cut a simple shape, such as a circle, from a sheet of paper-backed special paper. Fold it in half and draw another shape within it as shown. Cut out along your lines, being careful not to cut through the folded edge. Unfold the shapes and bend in different directions.

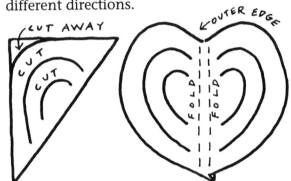

Circle fan: Cut a piece of special paper so that it is twice as long as it is wide. Fan-fold or accordion-fold the sheet. Staple or tie a string at the center. Spread it open into a circle. Paste the edges together.

Paper ball: Trace around a glass to make three equal circles. Lightly fold the circles in half, and then in half again, making fourths. Use the fold lines as guides to mark the slit locations as shown. Next, bend the sides of circle 1 and pass it through the slit in circle 2. Bend the edges of circle 2 and circle 1 and pass them through the slit in circle 3. Unfold the circles into a three-dimensional ball.

1. PASS CIRCLE 1 THROUGH SLIT OF CIRCLE 2.
2. PASS CIRCLE 1 AND 2 THROUGH CIRCLE 3 SLIT.
3. UNFOLD.

★ RECYCLED SCRAPS ★

Don't let those precious scraps of special paper go to waste. You can make crafts from even the smallest pieces.

WHAT YOU NEED

Special paper

Construction paper

Paper paste (page 77–78)

White glue

WHAT YOU DO

Magnets and buttons: Cut simple shapes (such as a star, duck, flower, or fish) from cardboard-backed, vinyl-covered special paper. Use white glue to attach a magnet to the back. Or, use white glue to attach a jewelry backing. Now both you and the refrigerator can look spiffy!

Collages: Pick a theme, such as spring. Cut spring shapes from special paper scraps such as birds, butterflies, and flowers from Bubble, Rainbow, or Marble paper. Paste them onto a piece of solid-colored construction paper.

Then & Now

Precious patches: Pioneer women never wasted a scrap of precious fabric. Even worn-out clothes were cut and pieced into quilt blankets. Your scraps of special paper are as precious as the cloth scraps of pioneer days. Cut and paste them onto construction paper in geometric quilt designs. Find a book at the library that shows quilt designs. Try imitating them with paper. Or, create your own patterns.

★ BATIK BANNER ★

ARTIST'S CHOICE!

Enjoy an art that's 2,000 years old and still in style! From African tribal shapes to Indian paisleys, batik cloth is found the world over. Keep parts of the cloth its original color; color the rest a new color. That's the basic idea of batik.

WHAT YOU NEED

Instant Flour Molding Paste (page 84)

Super See-Through Watercolor (page 15)

Cotton cloth — about 18 inches (117 cm) square. (Scraps of an old sheet work fine.)

Wooden dowels (2 inches or 5 cm longer than the width of the cloth)

White glue

Hanging string

Paper

Squeeze bottle

Paintbrush

WHAT YOU DO

1 Plan the batik by first sketching out a design on paper. Keep the design simple. Each line you draw represents where you will squeeze the paste. The paste will keep the fabric beneath it white. Colored areas will be between the lines.

2 It's helpful, but not essential, to work on a wooden board or piece of heavy, corrugated cardboard. Then you can use push-pins to hold the cloth in place on the work surface.

3 Fill the squeeze bottle with paste and squeeze out your design onto the cloth.

Remember, where you squeeze remains white. Let cloth dry overnight.

4 The next day, use watercolors to paint in the areas you want colored. When the paint has dried, crumble off the paste with your fingers.

5 Ask a grown-up to help you staple or glue dowels to the top and bottom edges of the batik. Leave an inch (2.5 cm) of wood on either side of the batik.

6 Tie a string onto the tips of the top dowel to hang banner.

Wearable art: Use commercial fabric paints if you'd like to batik a T-shirt or bandanna.

Bright colors: Use tempera (page 19) for a bold look. The tempera will dry hard, making the cloth stiff.

Crinkle-cloth: Use a blunt knife to spread the paste all over the cloth. Let the paste dry. Crumple the cloth into a ball to crack the paste. Lay the cloth flat and paint into the cracks. Let the paint dry. Scrape off the paste.

"TIK" MEANS DROP

What does "drop" have to do with batik? Everything, if we're talking about a drop of wax. You used flour paste to keep parts of your cloth white. The people of Indonesia use hot, melted wax. Wax is carefully poured onto the cloth to form beautiful images of fruits, flowers, birds, or butterflies. Next the fabric is dyed. The wax resists the dye, so when the wax is removed the image stays white against a colorful, dyed background.

★ WONDERFUL WANDS ★

Make a bouquet of colorful wands to brighten your home.

WHAT YOU NEED

Sticks (gathered from the ground only)

Tempera paint (page 19)

Yarn

Special paper scraps

Beads (see Jazzy Jewelry, page 59)

WHAT YOU DO

1 Find some nicely shaped sticks. They can be straight or have branches. You may leave the bark on or peel it off.

2 Paint the entire stick one background color. Let dry.

3 Paint stripes, dots, or other patterns on the stick. Let dry.

4 If your stick has branches, you can weave colored string among them. Knot one end of a string onto a branch. Wrap the string around another branch. Continue making a string web within the branches.

5 Display several wands in a jar or container covered with special paper (see page 132), or prop one up on your mantel or bookcase as a sculpture.

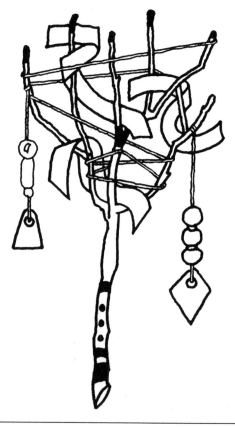

ARTIST'S CHOICE!

Soak cotton string in Super-See-Through Watercolors (page 15) for a natural look.

- - - - - - - - -

Leave some yarn hanging after making the final knots. String on beads or tie bits of special paper to the hanging ends.

- - - - - - - - -

Wrap different colors of yarn tightly around a single branch or branchless stick. Use the yarn to make bands of textured color on the wand.

THE WAND OF HERMES

In Greek mythology, the *caduceus* (kuh-doo-see-uhs) was the wand of Hermes, messenger of the Greek gods. The wand, made of olive wood and gold, was entwined with serpents (snakes). With his magical caduceus, the ancient Greeks believed Hermes possessed power over dreams and sleep. Today we see the caduceus used as the symbol for medical services.

STAINED GLASS ART

A PAINTING OF LIGHT

Imagine a painting made of light. That's really what a stained-glass window is. Light shines through colored pieces of glass creating a picture.

Stained-glass windows were probably first created about one thousand years ago — about the time of the discovery of glass in the Near East. These dramatic windows were popular in the Gothic cathedrals of the Middle Ages. The windows were not only beautiful, they were used to relate stories from the Bible.

To make a stained-glass window takes careful planning. First a drawing is made. Then the artist cuts small pieces of glass to fit the shapes drawn. Each piece is painted and then fired in a kiln (oven) to give it color. The pieces are held together with lead strips. Iron bars support each section. Then the entire window is installed in the wall.

★ WINDOW ART ★

You don't need to live in a cathedral to brighten your home with the colored light of a stained-glass window. Transform an ordinary window into beautiful (washable) stained glass, but please ask permission first.

WHAT YOU NEED

Smooth soap paint in several colors (page 32)

Flour finger paint (page 43)

Black powdered tempera

Paintbrush

Squeeze bottle

WHAT YOU DO

1 Plan your stained-glass painting on paper. Make a simple sketch of "lead" outlines and "colored glass" areas.

2 Add black powdered tempera to flour finger paint. It should be the consistency of mayonnaise. (If the paint is too thick and heavy, it will slide off the glass after it dries.) Place paint in a squeeze bottle. Experiment squeezing the paint out on a window away from your painting.

3 Make the outlines with the squeeze bottle. You may paint within a single pane of glass. Or, make a large outline of a shape to paint within. Let the outlines dry for a few hours.

4 Paint with colored soap paint within the outlined areas.

If you're like most painters, you probably love the way color brings art to life. Marc Chagall, a Russian-born artist who painted during the 1900s, loved the way sunlight affected color so much that he devoted the last years of his life to creating some of the most stunning stained-glass windows in the world. The Rose Window of the Metz Cathedral in France is perhaps his most famous stained-glass creation.

Like many artists, Chagall was fascinated by both the medium he chose and the message he wanted to give to those who would view his art. His stained-glass work often related Biblical stories — but always with some of his personal beliefs expressed within his art, too.

★ PLAYFUL PARACHUTE ★

LIFE-SAVING NYLON

What's made of nylon cloth and can slow a person falling from the sky, a race car making its final lap, and a capsule descending from space? You guessed it — a parachute. This umbrella-shaped device is neatly folded and placed into a small fabric pack. Pull the rip cord to open the pack and unfurl a giant wind resister that works wonderfully to slow down a rapid-moving object.

Sketched by artist Leonardo da Vinci five hundred years ago, the parachute has saved the life of many an aviator, especially during World War II.

Color the parachute with beautiful watercolors. Paint and attach the passenger. Throw it up in the air. It *won't* come crashing down!

WHAT YOU NEED

15" (97.5 cm) square napkin or lightweight sheeting cloth

Super See-Through Water-colors (page 15)

Clothespin

Basic Tempera (page 19)

4 2-foot (60 m) lengths of thread

Paintbrush

WHAT YOU DO

1 Unfold the napkin. Refold as shown. Dip the corners and edges into a bowl of water-color. Or color the cloth with bright dabs of watercolor.

2 Paint the clothespin to look like a person, following the directions on page 26.

3 Knot a thread onto each corner of the napkin.

4 Tie the loose ends of the threads together; then tie them around the top of the clothespin.

5 Fold and roll the napkin as shown.

6 Stand on a chair and toss up high. Watch how the napkin resists the fall of the clothespin passenger.

Then & Now

Swedish cookie stamps: Long ago in Sweden, it was the custom for guests to receive a cookie stamped with the host's unique design. Families had a set of custom stamps to use when baking cookies for holiday celebrations. These stamps, carved in wood or dry clay, were pressed into the dough before baking. The result was a very artistic cookie embossed with birds, hearts, animals, or other intricate patterns. Some stamps have been passed down from generation to generation and are still in use today. If you go to Sweden, you might be lucky enough to eat a cookie stamped with a 200-year-old design!

Would you like to create a cookie stamp of your own? Prepare your favorite gingerbread cookie or sugar cookie dough. Break off small balls of dough and flatten in your hands. Place on cookie sheets and either make a design in the dough with a toothpick or press in a fancy button print (wash it thoroughly first) in all the cookies. Put button away when you are done. Bake and then serve your stamped cookies to your friends and family.

★ CUSTOM STAMP ★

Make your mark with a stamp design all your own.

WHAT YOU NEED

Flour dough (page 46)

Tempera paint (page 19)

ARTIST'S CHOICE!

Make a one-inch-thick (2.5 cm) disc. Use your fingers or small objects to make impressions in the disc.

- - - - - - - - - - - - - - -

Make one-inch-thick (2.5 cm) shapes: hearts, diamonds, circles, and squares. Stamp out these simple shapes in an interesting pattern.

WHAT YOU DO

1. Make a disc from the dough about half an inch (1 cm) thick. (Any simple, flat shape such as a circle, heart, or triangle will work.)

2. Roll out some coils, also about half an inch (1 cm) thick.

3. Place the coils onto the disc in an interesting pattern.

4. When you are satisfied with the pattern, turn the disc over and lightly press the stamp on the table to level it. The parts of the design that touch the table are the parts that will print.

5. Let the stamp dry for several days. Level the stamp (step 4) every so often as it dries.

6. Ready to print? Place some tempera on a paper plate. Dip the stamp into the paint. Print on paper.

★ PAPER JEWELRY ★

TORN PAPER PIECES

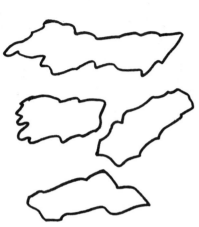

Wear unique jewelry made of handmade paper and paint. Cut or tear, paint or paste — that's all it takes.

WHAT YOU NEED

A variety of handmade papers (page 90)

Several colors of Doughy Paint (page 29)

Colored construction paper

White glue or hot glue

Jewelry backings such as earring posts, barrette clasp, or pin backing

WHAT YOU DO

1 Tear or cut an interesting shape from a sheet of thick, handmade paper to be the base of your piece of jewelry. (Be sure the torn paper is larger than the jewelry backing.)

2 Now tear or cut smaller pieces of other handmade papers. Arrange them in an interesting pattern on the paper base. Glue them in place. Let dry.

3 Squeeze doughy paint on top of your paper arrangement. Add interesting little designs. Let dry.

4 Attach the paper base to the jewelry backing with white glue. Or, ask a grown-up to help you use hot glue. Let dry.

5 Put on your original jewelry and be ready for all those compliments!

ARTIST'S CHOICE!

Use the combination of handmade paper and doughy paint to decorate greeting cards or covered boxes.

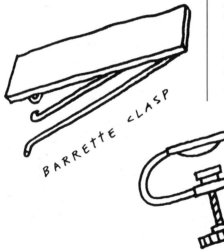

BARRETTE CLASP

TIE CLASP

EARRING POST

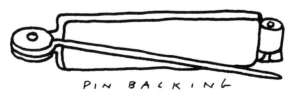

PIN BACKING

APPENDIX A

CREATIVE ART GUIDELINES FOR PARENTS, TEACHERS, & CAREGIVERS

Encourage every child to express his or her individuality through art. As much as possible, allow each child's imagination to take flight. Making art concoctions is an inspiring way for all children to react to their impressions of the medium they concoct. Maybe the watercolors run together, reminding them of a rainbow; perhaps mixing up a special dough sparks the idea for a particular sculpture. The goal is creative exploration, not a particular outcome. There's no right, wrong, or better way to use the medium.

THE MEDIUM IS THE MESSAGE

Each concoction has a look and feel all its own. Invite children to tune in to what is unique about each medium. Experiment with the paint, dough, or clay to see what it can do. Then create a product inspired by the medium. Michelangelo did not decide on his subject and then set out to find the appropriate stone. Instead, it was the stone that inspired the subject. He selected his blocks for the figures he perceived to be within them. Many contemporary artists are more interested in what the medium can do than how the finished product looks.

IT'S THE REAL THING

Realistic representation isn't taught by showing children your own model. Instead, show them the real thing. For example, bring a cat into the classroom. Let it roam and nap among the children. Let everyone feel its soft fur. Talk about how it looks, feels, and behaves. Now pass out the art materials as the cat looks on. The result will be images that say "cat" loud and clear in thirty different ways. On the other hand, if you present a picture you've painted of a cat to the class, you'll have thirty cat pictures that all look like yours.

Bring in still life, let the children be models, venture out into the school yard. Talk about what you see. Then pass out the materials to concoct paint, dough, paper, and paste. Help children really see and express their world in their own way.

LEARN FROM THE MASTERS

While there's a time for free creative exploration, there's also a time to learn from others. Picasso studied the works of his predecessors before breaking traditions of the past and creating his own. Bring the works of great artists into your home or the classroom. Talk about their approach, what they were trying to achieve and communicate, and why they used a certain medium.

Have children experience and learn from the approach, not duplicate the masterpiece. Use thick paints (page 27) like Van Gogh, responding to the paint itself, not to what Van Gogh chose to paint. Or, look at a Chagall stained-glass window and attempt to communicate the same feeling using whatever mediums are available, not try to do a stained-glass-styled window.

SEE THE WORLD

Share folk art from around the world. Libraries are filled with books of photographs of the treasures from King Tut's tomb or pottery from villages in Africa and Latin America. Children gain understanding and appreciation of a culture by creating crafts in its tradition. Again, children shouldn't copy a particular craft object. Invite them to make the craft in their own way while experiencing traditional techniques and the spirit of the culture. See Alexandra Terzian's *The Kids' Multicultural Art Book* (Williamson Publishing).

DRESS THE PART

Encourage children to wear old clothes or have big, old smock shirts available. Cover work areas you care about with newspaper or work outdoors. Art and the creative process can get messy, and children should not feel inhibited as they work with various mediums.

RESPECT THE RESULTS

If you follow the preceding guidelines, you'll end up with an incredibly rich and varied collection of children's art. Celebrate the uniqueness of each piece. Encourage children to respect the differences in their approaches. Children can often be less accepting of differences than grown-ups. The best affirmation you can offer is to display all art work, rotating the pieces, if you lack space. Classroom art work is meant to be seen and enjoyed by everyone in the classroom community. And art work at home is meant to be displayed, too.

APPENDIX B

CONCOCTING ACROSS THE CURRICULUM

HANDS-ON LEARNING

Children learn best when they experience information first hand. As an instructional tool, passive listening just can't compete with physical "doing." Measuring, mixing, and then working with the concoctions they've created, brings learning to life. Children don't simply hear about the physical properties of dough, they feel it and know from experience how kneading changes those properties.

From there, children get to solidify their experiences with something concrete — a creative art work representative of who they are, how they feel, how they respond to the medium, and their understanding of what each medium can be used for. This creative understanding can be as subtle as deciding to use sawdust dough or salt dough for a particular sculpture, or it can be as dramatic as choosing to express their feelings about the loss of a pet with bold Almost-Oil Soap Paint or subtle shades of watercolors.

SMALL GROUPS WORK BEST

Classroom concocting works best in small groups — at a supervised learning center or as one of several activity stations. Let children get as close to the concocting process as possible. The more each child can actually measure and mix to make the mixture, the more the mystery of concocting will mean.

If this isn't possible, the teacher can mix up a sample batch as children watch (as opposed to making everything in advance). Once a few guidelines for working with the substance are given, and a project is suggested, encourage children to take their cues from the substance itself and their own imaginations as they work their mixture into an original creation.

CROSS-CURRICULAR LEARNING

Concoction-making can be a powerful thread that weaves across the curriculum into children's lives. Here is a sampling of how making concoctions can cross academic disciplines from science to math to literature; can cross cultures, religions, and time; can cross modes of self-expression in music, art, and poetry.

★ How gluten releases in dough by feeling the dough hold together while kneading

★ How colors combine to make new colors

★ How pigment plus binder forms paint by blending them together, and how ancient cultures discovered this property

★ About the art and science of making handmade papers by learning of the properties of cellulose fiber

★ About the adhesive properties of gelatin, gluten, and sugar by mixing their own pastes from these substances

★ About soil differences in sand, mud, and clay

★ How to measure accurately and read carefully by making mediums dependent on these skills

★ How people discovered clays, pastes, papers, and paints by combining ingredients from nature

★ How people used nature and art to express their fears about the unknown, such as painting their bodies or making Zuni fetishes to bring hunting success or ward off evil

★ How proportion and ratio can alter a concoction's properties and artistic applications

★ How interconnected everything we do is with our past and the future by studying soils for concoctions and discovering a lot about biology, geology, and archaeology

★ How trial and error are necessary in all attempts at discovery and creativity

★ The inventive spirit of men and women to create what they need with what they have at hand.

EXTENDING LEARNING

To extend learning to other areas, we must be open to the directions the children are drawn to. Groups can be formed to explore and investigate certain issues and subjects raised. All of this becomes meaningful on multiple levels as students are motivated from their initial hands-on experience, and you, as their facilitator, encourage them in their continuing discovery of themselves and their world.

INDEX TO CONCOCTION RECIPES

INDEX TO TECHNIQUES

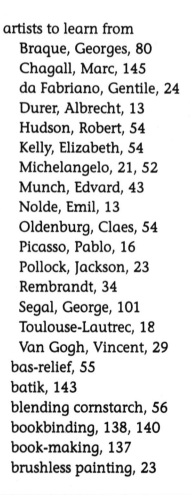

INDEX
TO ART & CRAFT ACTIVITIES

INDEX

TO ART & CRAFT ACTIVITIES

MORE KIDS' BOOKS FROM
WILLIAMSON PUBLISHING

*To order additional copies of Kids' Crazy Concoctions,
please enclose $12.95 per copy plus $2.50 for shipping. Follow
"To Order" instructions on the last page. Thank you.*

Winner of the Stepping Stones Environmental Award!

EcoArt!
Earth-Friendly Art & Craft Experiences for 3- to 9-year-olds
by Laurie Carlson

What better way to learn to love and care for the Earth than through creative art play! Laurie Carlson's latest book is packed with 150 projects using only recyclable, reusable, or nature's own found-art materials. These fabulous activities are sure to please any child!

160 pages, 11 x 8 1/2, 400 illustrations
Quality paperback, $12.95

Winner of the Parents' Choice Gold Award!

THE KIDS' MULTICULTURAL ART BOOK
Art & Craft Experiences from Around the World
by Alexandra M. Terzian

Alexandra Terzian brings an unsurpassed enthusiasm to the hands-on multicultural art experience. Children will reach across continents and oceans with paper, paste, and paints, while absorbing basic sensibilities about the wondrous cultures of others. Children will learn by making such things as the *Korhogo Mud Cloth* from Africa, the *Chippewa Dream Catcher* of the American Indian, the *Kokeshi Doll* of Japan, *Chinese Egg Painting*, the *Mexican Folk Art Tree of Life*, and the *Twirling Palm Puppet* from India. A virtual feast of multicultural art and craft experiences!

160 pages, 11 x 8 1/2, over 400 how-to-do-it illustrations
Quality paperback, $12.95

KIDS COOK!
Fabulous Food for the Whole Family
by Sarah Williamson and Zachary Williamson

Here's a cookbook written for kids by two teenagers who know what kids like to eat! Filled with over 150 recipes for great tasting foods that kids ages 6 and up can cook for themselves and for their families and friends, too. Try breakfast bonanzas like *Breakfast Sundaes*, great lunches including *Chicken Shirt Pocket*, super salads like *A Whale of a Fruit Salad*, quick snacks and easy extras like *Nacho Nibbles*, delicious dinners including *Pizza Originale*, and dynamite desserts and soda fountain treats including *Chocolate Surprise Cupcakes*. All recipes are for "real," healthy foods — not cutesy recipes that are no fun to eat. One terrific book!

176 pages, 11 x 8 1/2, over 150 recipes, illustrations
Quality paperback, $12.95

THE KIDS' SCIENCE BOOK
Creative Experiences for Hands-On Fun
by Robert Hirschfeld and Nancy White

Science has never been so accessible to the hearts and minds of kids before! Learning and hands-on fun are one and the same as kids explore the human body and make a model lung; use levers to make a jumping coin game; discover the world of spiders while making an amazing climbing spider; plus learn about plants, color, the five senses, planet earth, magnets, and water and air pressure. *The Kids' Science Book* is crammed with ideas that pique kids' curiosity and with creative activities to solidify the learning experience.

160 pages, 11 x 8 1/2, 70 activities; over 150 illustrations
Quality paperback, $12.95

KIDS MAKE MUSIC!
Clapping and Tapping from Bach to Rock
by Avery Hart and Paul Mantell

No instruments necessary — just hands, feet, and wiggly bodies! Kids are natural music makers, and with the kid-loving music makers, Avery Hart and Paul Mantell, children everywhere will be doing the *Dinosaur Dance*, singing the *Dishwashin' Blues*, cleaning their rooms to *Rap*, belting it out in a *Jug Band* or An *Accidental Orchestra*, putting on a *Fairy Tale Opera*, learning to *Tap Dance*, or creating a *Bona Fide Ballet* (homemade tutu included)! Those hands will be clapping, those feet will be tapping, those faces will be grinning, and they may be humming anything from Bach to Rock.

160 pages, 11 x 8^1/$_2$, with hundreds of illustrations
Quality paperback, $12.95

TALES ALIVE!
Ten Multicultural Folktales with Activities
by Susan Milord

Award-winning author Susan Milord brings ten folktales from around the world to life with a myriad of exciting, relevant hands-on activities. *Tales Alive!* will lock these universal stories into the hearts and minds of children for many years to follow. Includes wondrous stories from Australia, Argentina, China, Ghana, Canada, Russia, and other countries. A virtual feast of multicultural fun and learning!

128 pages, 8^1/$_2$ x 11, full-color illustrations
Quality paperback, $15.95

THE LITTLE HANDS ART BOOK
Exploring Arts & Crafts with 2- to 6-year-olds
by Judy Press

The perfect introductory art book for little hands with lots to express. Author Judy Press has an uncanny understanding of how to encourage the creative spirit in all children. Over 70 unusual crafts including paper bag picnic basket, muffin cup birds, milk carton caboose, egg carton caterpillar, dough porcupine, and Popsicle stick flower gardens. Every child is certain to flourish as little hands are given the freedom to express themselves in the most amazing ways!

160 pages, 8^1/$_2$ x 11, over 150 illustrations
Quality paperback, $12.95

THE KIDS' WILDLIFE BOOK
Exploring Animal Worlds through Indoor/Outdoor Experiences
by Warner Shedd

Introduce children to the wildlife of North America from toads to timber wolves, bats to bobcats, owls to armadillos. With awesome tales, facts, and amusing anecdotes to make the 100-plus activities meaningful and fun, Warner Shedd's thoughtful approach fills children with wonder and respect for the creatures with whom they share this planet.

160 pages, 11 x 8^1/$_2$, with illustrations, range maps, index
Quality paperback, $12.95

GREAT PARTIES FOR KIDS
35 Celebrations for Toddlers to Preteens
by Nancy Fyke, Lynn Nejam, Vicki Overstreet

Celebrating birthdays, holidays, and just plain special days in the kid-loving spirit of fun and excitement has never been so easy! Here are 35 sure-to-please parties that cover everything from clever party themes to creating invitations, decorations, and low-cost party favors, to party games and activities, to over 40 recipes for kid-pleasing party foods. So join in the fun. It's party time!

128 pages, 8 x 10, illustrations
Quality paperback, $10.95

HANDS AROUND THE WORLD
365 Creative Ways to Build Cultural Awareness & Global Respect
by Susan Milord

Award-winning author Susan Milord invites children to experience, taste, and embrace the daily lives of children from the far corners of the earth. In 365 days of experiences, it tears down stereotypes and replaces them with the fascinating realities of our differences and our similarities. Children everywhere can plant and grow, write and tell stories, draw and craft, cook and eat, sing and dance, look and explore, as they learn to live in an atmosphere of global respect and cultural awareness that is born of personal experience.

160 pages, 11 x 8$^{1}/_{2}$, over 400 illustrations
Quality paperback, $12.95

Over 200,000 copies sold!

THE KIDS' NATURE BOOK
365 Indoor/Outdoor Activities and Experiences
by Susan Milord

Winner of the Parents' Choice Gold Award for learning and doing books, The *Kids' Nature Book* is loved by children, grandparents, and friends alike. Simple projects and activities emphasize fun while quietly reinforcing the wonder of the world we all share.

Packed with facts and fun!
160 pages, 11 x 8$^{1}/_{2}$, 425 illustrations
Quality paperback, $12.95

Over 250,000 copies sold!

KIDS CREATE!
Art & Craft Experiences for 3- to 9-year-olds
by Laurie Carlson

What's the most important experience for children ages 3 to 9? Why, to create something by themselves. Carlson provides over 150 creative experiences ranging from making dinosaur sculptures to clay cactus gardens, from butterfly puppets to windsocks. Plenty of help for the parents working with the kids, too! A delightfully innovative book.

160 pages, 11 x 8$^{1}/_{2}$, over 400 illustrations
Quality paperback, $12.95

KIDS LEARN AMERICA!
Bringing Geography to Life with People, Places, & History
by Patricia Gordon and Reed C. Snow

This creative and exciting book is about making every region of our country come alive from within, about being connected to the earth and the people across this great expanse called America. Let us all join together — kids, parents, friends, teachers, grandparents — and put America, its geography, its history, and its heritage back on the map!

176 pages, 11 x 8¹/2, maps, illustrations
Quality paperback, $12.95

ADVENTURES IN ART
Art & Craft Experiences for 7- to 14-year-olds
by Susan Milord

Imagine an art book that encourages children to explore, to experience, to touch and to see, to learn and to create...imagine a true adventure in art. Here's a book that teaches artisans' skills without stifling creativity. Covers making handmade papers, puppets, masks, paper seascapes, seed art, tin can lantern, berry ink, still life, silk screen, batiking, carving, and so much more. Perfect for the older child. Let the adventure begin!

160 pages, 11 x 8¹/2, 500 illustrations
Quality paperback, $12.95

KIDS AND WEEKENDS!
Creative Ways to Make Special Days
by Avery Hart and Paul Mantell

Packed with truly creative ways to play, have fun, learn, grow, and build self-esteem and positive relationships. Transform some part of every weekend — even if it is only 30 minutes — into a special experience. Everything from backyard nature to putting on a magic show to creating a bird sanctuary to writing a book about yourself to environmentally-sound activities indoors and out. Whatever your interests, no matter how busy you are, kids will savor special weekend moments.

176 pages, 11 x 8¹/2, over 400 illustrations
Quality paperback, $12.95

Also by Jill Hauser

GROWING UP READING
Learning to Read through Creative Play
by Jill Frankel Hauser

Here's the breakthrough that ushers young children into the fantastic world of reading — through play! Hauser shows busy parents how to make learning to read part of early childhood —just like learning to walk and talk are. Playful exploration is the natural way children learn, and with the author's fun-filled materials and ideas, you and your children will discover the fun of learning to read while sharing special times together.

144 pages, 8¹/2 x 11, index
Quality paperback, $12.95

To Order:

At your bookstore or order directly from Williamson Publishing. We accept Visa and MasterCard (please include number and expiration date), or send check to:

**Williamson Publishing Company
Church Hill Road, P.O. Box 185
Charlotte, Vermont 05445**

Toll-Free phone orders with credit cards:
1-800-234-8791

Please add $2.50 for postage per total order. Satisfaction is guaranteed or full refund without questions or quibbles.

* Please note: Prices may be slightly higher in Canada.